Sarah Forbes Bonetta

Sarah Forbes Bonetta

Queen Victoria's African Princess

JOHN VAN DER KISTE

A & F

First published by A & F 2018

Copyright © 2018 John Van der Kiste
All rights reserved

A & F Publications,
South Brent, Devon, England TQ10 9AS

Typeset 11pt Georgia

ISBN-13: 978-1719186377
ISBN-10: 1719186375

Cover photograph: Sarah Forbes Bonetta, 1862

Printed by CreateSpace

CONTENTS

Illustrations	3
Timeline	5
Introduction	7
1. Lieutenant-Commander Forbes in Dahomey	17
2. Sarah in England	31
3. Sarah returns to Africa	45
4. Sarah returns to England	61
5. Sarah's marriage	72
6. Mrs Davies in Africa	91
Afterword	106
Acknowledgements	111
Reference Notes	112
Bibliography	115
Index	118

ILLUSTRATIONS

Map of Dahomey	19
The procession of *Ek-onee-noo-ah-toh*	27
King Gezo of Dahomey	28
Sarah Forbes Bonetta, c.1849	29
Sarah Forbes Bonetta, c.1849	30
Queen Victoria and Prince Albert, 1854	43
Sir Charles Phipps, c.1860	44
The Reverend Henry Venn	59
An African school	60
Princess Alice, 1856	70
Sarah Forbes Bonetta, 1856	71
Sarah Forbes Bonetta, 1862	85
Sarah Forbes Bonetta, 1862	86
The wedding of Sarah and James Davies, 1862	87
St Nicholas Church, Brighton	88
Sarah and James Davies, 1862	89
Sarah and James Davies, 1862	90
Bishop Samuel Ajayi Crowther, 1867	101
Queen Victoria and Princess Beatrice, c.1880	102
Funchal, Madeira	104
The English cemetery at Funchal	105
Victoria Randle and her children	110

TIMELINE

1807
Slave Trade Act (An Act for the Abolition of the Slave Trade), prohibiting the slave trade in the British Empire, passed by Parliament

1833
Slavery Abolition Act, abolishing slavery in the British Empire, passed by Parliament

c.1843
Aina born at Okeadon

1849-50
HMS *Bonetta* arrives at Dahomey; Aina rescued by Lieutenant-Commander Forbes and renamed Sarah Forbes Bonetta, taken to England, meets Queen Victoria for the first time, and settles at Gillingham with Forbes family

1851
Sarah returns to Africa, and is educated in Sierra Leone; death of Forbes, and publication of *Dahomey and the Dahomans*

1855
Sarah returns to England; settles at Gillingham with Schoen family

1860
Sarah settles at Brighton with Miss Welsh

1862
Sarah marries James Davies in Brighton, 14 August, and returns to Africa

1863
Victoria Davies born

1871
Arthur Davies born

1873
Stella Davies born

c.1879
Sarah develops tuberculosis and goes to Madeira

1880
Sarah dies, 15 August

1889
James Davies remarries

1906
James Davies dies, 29 April

INTRODUCTION

Sarah Forbes Bonetta 'discovered'

On Christmas Day 2017, several million viewers tuned into watch a special festive episode of *Victoria*, the television drama series starring Jenna Coleman, created by Daisy Goodwin and based on the Queen's life. The programme was based partly around an episode in Queen Victoria's family history that has almost completely, and rather surprisingly, escaped the attention of several generations of biographers and historians.

As Jenna Coleman explained, Sarah, the girl who has come to be recognised as 'Queen Victoria's African Princess', entered the Queen's life in 1850 as an orphan, abandoned and alone, and she believed that the monarch could 'see something of herself in her. It becomes an almost cathartic experience. By trying to help Sarah rebuild herself, Victoria eases the wounds of her own childhood companion.'[1]

Daisy Goodwin saw the relationship between the Queen and Sarah as 'thoroughly modern' in that the sovereign had no prejudices at all, saw people as her subjects, did not discriminate between them, and in this context was surprisingly broad-minded as well as modern. In the programme, she said, she was trying to show that she saw a little girl who was a princess and had lost her family, and wanted to show how a princess should be treated. The Queen was 'trying to mend the wounds of her past', while Prince Albert was questioning her whether she was really thinking about the child, or about herself?[2]

Readers of substantial lives of the sovereign written and published by Elizabeth Longford (1964), Mrs Cecil Woodham-Smith (1972), Stanley Weintraub (1987), Giles St Aubyn (1991), Christopher Hibbert (2001), and A.N. Wilson (2014) will search the texts and indexes in vain for even the slightest reference to Sarah Forbes Bonetta, or 'Sally', as the Queen called her. It is remarkable that such an unusual yet significant episode should have been completely neglected.

The person to whom the story of Sarah Forbes Bonetta owes everything, or almost everything, was Walter Dean Myers, a prolific American author who lived in New Jersey. Towards the end of the twentieth century, he came across a batch of letters concerning a young girl who had lived in England during the Victorian era. The material was listed in a catalogue of books and ephemera that had been sent to him from London. In his own words, having 'been on wild goose chases' before, he approached the material with caution. He went to look at the papers, and then corroborated the basic facts with an account of her rescue in a book written and published at around the time by Frederick E. Forbes, the man who had rescued her from almost certain death.

It proved to him that everything that he had read was absolutely genuine. At the same time, he had been put on the trail of an almost hitherto completely undocumented episode in Victorian history. Consultation with the staff at the Royal Archives, Windsor Castle, led to his writing and publishing a short biography, *At Her Majesty's Request* (1999), written primarily with an intended readership of ages

9-12. It formed the basis of an article in the monthly journal *Royalty Digest* by Shelby Morrison the following year, and an entry in Helen Rappaport's *Queen Victoria: A Biographical Companion* (2003). Sarah was also featured prominently in *Black and British – A Forgotten History*, a four-part BBC TV series presented by historian David Olusoga and broadcast in the autumn of 2016.

There are scattered details about the life of Sarah Forbes Bonetta on various websites, including a few short references in the Queen's complete online journals. Extracts from these journals had been published together with selections from her letters in nine volumes between 1907 and 1932, but in these there is not a single mention of Sarah to be found. Otherwise remarkably little is to be discovered. Apart from the correspondence acquired by Myers, there is an almost total absence of primary sources.

Employment of Africans, Indians and others at the royal court is one thing. But the story of Sarah, the orphan who was literally given as a present to Queen Victoria, is quite another.

The royal family, court and 'people of colour'

Queen Victoria and most of her family were renowned for their lack, even abhorrence, of racial prejudice. In her later years the monarch was notable for her stout defence of her loyal Indian servant Abdul Karim, 'the Munshi', and of Indian culture in general. He was resented by several of her children, though not reasons of race but more as he was an unscrupulous individual who regularly took advantage of his privileged position and foremost royal protector. She found it necessary on occasion to instruct those around her that the Indians in her service must never be referred to as 'black men' and her Prime Minister Lord Salisbury were among those who had to apologise for what in the nineteenth century was regarded as a commonplace error. Even some of the more liberal personalities at court, like her Private Secretary Sir Henry Ponsonby, were known to refer disparagingly to the 'Black Brigade'.

Queen Victoria's son and heir, later King Edward VII, shared her total lack of racial prejudice wholeheartedly. While he and his suite were on a visit to India in 1875, he was astonished and appalled to find that most of the British lived in splendour while the impoverished Indian population clearly did not. When some of his entourage tried to belittle his concerns, he told them in no uncertain terms that because a man had a different coloured face and religion from theirs, 'there is no reason why he should be treated as a brute'. Among the few people who really disliked him were British officials in the Indian sub-continent who resented his efforts to undermine their authority by complaining to the government in London of their 'rude and rough manner' towards the native population. Six years later he was with King Kalakaua of Hawaii at a garden party in England, and insisted on his guest's being accorded precedence over his brother-in-law the German Crown Prince Frederick William, later Emperor Frederick III. When the latter protested, the Prince silenced him with a retort of 'Either the brute is a King, or he's a common or garden n-----; and, if the latter, what's he doing here?'[3] In present day terms, such a remark would be regarded as irredeemably racist, but in 1881 it was considered perfectly acceptable.

After Edward came to the throne critics would scoff at him behind his back as 'vulgar', because he abhorred racism and anti-Semitism. He did however send the Munshi back to India, not for discriminatory reasons, but rather because he disliked and trusted the man whom he considered untrustworthy and an unprincipled opportunist.

The attitude of him and his mother was in stark contrast to his rather less enlightened grandson, later King Edward VIII, who wrote to his mistress Freda Dudley Ward after a visit to Barbados that he thought the 'coloured population' were 'revolting'. He proved the exception to the rule, with the rest of the family sharing the more enlightened views of his grandfather and great-grandmother, and indeed of successive generations. In 2017 a new personal assistant was selected by Queen Elizabeth II to become the first black equerry in British history. It was announced that Major Nana Kofi Twumasi-Ankrah, a Ghanaian-born officer who fought in the Afghanistan war, would fill one of the most important roles in the royal household. As an equerry, Major Twumasi-Ankrah, known as 'TA' to his friends, would act as one of the Queen's most-trusted attendants, his duties including assisting her with official engagements and welcoming high profile guests to royal residences.

Sir Henry Ponsonby and others may not have been aware that during the 'slave trade era', roughly from the beginning of the sixteenth century until abolition in 1833, the English court had a long history of employing black people, or 'blackamoors' as they were once known, a term later regarded as offensive. It is difficult to be sure who was the first, but it has been established that Catalina de Cardoneso arrived in England in 1501 with Catherine of Aragon, who had come to be betrothed to King Henry VII's eldest son Arthur, Prince of Wales, who died young with the result that Catherine later became Queen and the first of the six wives of his brother, subsequently King Henry VIII. Catalina served her mistress for twenty-six years as Lady of the Bedchamber.

She was not alone among her race, for others at court in Tudor times included John Blanke, the 'blacke trumpeter', employed by Kings Henry VII and Henry VIII between 1506 and 1512 at a wage of eightpence a day. He had a prominent role in the Westminster Tournament celebrations of 1511 that were staged to mark the birth of another royal Henry, Duke of Cornwall, the first son of Catherine of Aragon and Henry VIII who however only lived for six weeks. Blanke was mentioned twice on the Westminster Tournament Roll, a contemporary manuscript showing the procession to and from Westminster Abbey.

Elizabeth I had an African boy in her personal entourage. In a warrant dated 14 April 1574, it stated that the Queen ordered the clothes-maker Henry Henre to make him a 'garcon coat ... of white taphata cutt and lined ... striped with gold and silver with buckeram bayes ... knitted stockings [and] white shoes'. A few years after this, an increase in the black population of London led to calls for a royal proclamation to arrest and expel all *'negroes and blackamores'* from the kingdom. Modern research, however, has established that despite two letters being drafted by the Privy Council in 1596 and 1601 to this end, they were never promulgated and the envisaged mass expulsion never became official policy.

Among the most famous black servants at the British court were King George I's two Turkish Grooms of the Chamber, ha and a young black youth. There are no records about the latter, but the two former, Mehemet and Mustapha, were taken from Turkey as war captives and employed by George, Elector of Hanover and subsequently King of England. They lived as royal servants, performing various domestic and financial duties, including that of groom, Keeper of the Closet, Personal Treasurer, and Master of the Robes and more. Mehemet died at Kensington Palace in 1726, aged sixty-six, one year before his royal master. Mustapha lived another twelve years and died in Hanover.

African (and Turkish servants) during the slave trade years were one thing, but for an orphaned African to be presented to royalty was quite another. The story of Sarah Forbes Bonetta was therefore quite unique.

Royal ancestry of colour

Queen Victoria had a small degree of such ancestry herself through her grandmother Queen Charlotte. The consort of George III could trace her line of descent from Margarita de Castro e Souza, a Portuguese noblewoman of the fifteenth century. Her ancestors included King Alfonso III of Portugal, who reigned from 1248 to 1279, and one of his mistresses, Madragana, a Moor and thus a black African. In the thirteenth century, King Alfonso invaded and conquered Faro, a small town in the Algarve region of present-day southern Portugal, demanded the governor's daughter as a paramour, and had three children with her. One of their sons, Martin Alfonso, married into the noble de Souza family, who also had black ancestry, and Queen Charlotte therefore had African blood from both families. (The same can also be said of several other European royal families).

There is a theory that historians are unsure of Madragana's ethnicity. She may have been a Mozarab or Iberian Christian, and the remarks about her may be ascribed to a cruel and racist alignment between 'black' and 'ugly'. The Queen was mocked behind her back as particularly unattractive by eighteenth century standards, although it could be said that none of the

Hanoverian Queens Consort were exactly striking beauties.

The Scottish painter Allan Ramsay was a fervent supporter of the anti-slave trade movement, and his portrait of the Queen was said to have emphasised her 'mulatto' appearance. The royal physician, Baron Christian Friedrich Stockmar, described her as 'small and crooked, with a true mulatto face', while the novelist Sir Walter Scott wrote that she was ill-coloured' and disparagingly called her family 'a bunch of ill-coloured orangutans',[4] and one of the Prime Ministers commented of her that her nose was too wide and her lips too thick.

There may have been a similar episode of non-white blood in the French court a hundred years earlier. In November 1664 Princess Marie Anne, second daughter of King Louis XIV and Queen Maria Theresa, was born prematurely. She was rumoured to have been a black child, maybe fathered by Nabo, the Queen's African dwarf at court. Other contemporary accounts said that she was not black but 'very dark', perhaps purple, suffering from oxygen deprivation that commonly affected premature babies, and she died six weeks later. If true, this would give the lie to malicious gossips who said that the King had hidden her away as she had been unfaithful with a black man.

People of colour in Victorian Britain and the empire, and racial attitudes

The aftermath of the Napoleonic wars saw a number of groups of black soldiers and seaman settling in London, but this immigration was balanced after the slave trade was abolished completely, with fewer people arriving into the capital from the West Indies and Africa. Towards the middle of the century, there were some temporary restrictions on people coming from Africa. A few years later there was another wave of arrivals, forming small groups of black dockside communities in the Canning Town area of London, Cardiff and Liverpool, as a result of new shipping links established with the Caribbean and West Africa.

With people settling in Britain there was inevitably some racial prejudice and discrimination on a small scale in Victorian England. But it never prevented several nineteenth-century black people living in England from making a name for themselves in public life, commerce or the arts. One of these was Pablo Fanque, born William Darby in Norwich, who became an equestrian performer and circus proprietor of one of Britain's most successful nineteenth-century circuses, and was later immortalised by name in The Beatles' song 'Being for the Benefit of Mr. Kite!' Another was Nathaniel Wells, the son of a Welsh merchant and slave trader who settled in St Kitts, and a black slave from the island. After his father's death he was freed, inherited a fortune, moved to Monmouthshire and became Sheriff of the county, the first black man in Britain to hold such a position, in 1818. In the latter years of the century **Samuel Coleridge-Taylor,** son of a physician from Sierra Leone who settled in London, became England's first successful black composer and conductor. In the course of his work, his path would cross with that of Sarah's daughter. The first black Member of Parliament to take his seat at Westminster was the Anglo-Indian David Ochterlony Dyce Sombre, a Radical-Liberal, elected for Sudbury in 1841 but disenfranchised for corruption the following year. Not until the 1890s were any more British Indian members elected to serve.

Throughout the empire, the British upper classes tended to be almost invariably the least racist; it has been said that they suffered from a colour-blindness of sorts. West African tribal chiefs and Indian princes were often understood as the social equivalent of English gentlemen, and British rulers were often amused at the inability of lower-class white settlers to accept that aristocratic breeding cut across differences of colour. Lady Gordon, the wife of Sir Arthur Hamilton-Gordon, Governor of Fiji from 1875 to 1880, thought the native high-ranking Fijians 'such an undoubted aristocracy'. Their manners, she wrote, were 'so perfectly easy and well bred ... Nurse can't understand it at all, she looks down on them as an inferior race. I don't like to tell her that these ladies are my equals, which she is not!'[5]

Although her presence in England must have excited some curiosity, albeit in an age when the press was far less intrusive than it is today, the life of Sarah Forbes Bonetta while she was in England was certainly free of racial prejudice. Nevertheless her life between England, Africa and back again an almost bewildering number of times, under the protection of Queen Victoria, was a well-cosseted one in which for the most part she was carefully shielded from the outside world – and sometimes uncomfortably, not always happily so.

CHAPTER 1

Lieutenant-Commander Forbes in Dahomey

On 25 March 1807 the Slave Trade Act was passed by the British Parliament at Westminster, making the slave trade illegal throughout the British Empire. Once this was enacted, British campaigners directed their efforts towards encouraging those in France and the British colonies to do likewise. It resulted in the Slavery Abolition Act of 1833 which finally abolished the practice throughout the British Empire with the exceptions 'of the Territories in the Possession of the East India Company', namely Ceylon, later Sri Lanka, and St Helena, these exceptions following suit in 1843. However, during the first half of the nineteenth century, efforts still constantly needed to be made to eliminate the practice in Africa.

In 1808 the British Royal Navy established the West Africa Squadron in order to patrol the coast of West Africa and therefore suppress the Atlantic slave trade. Based at Portsmouth, it employed around a sixth of the Royal Navy fleet and marines. In 1819 the Navy established a West Coast of Africa Station, and the West Africa Squadron was subsequently renamed the Preventative Squadron. Between 1808 and 1860 it captured 1,600 slave ships and freed about 150,000 Africans who were aboard their vessels. It also took action against African leaders who refused to agree to British treaties to outlaw the trade. Some were more compliant than others, and anti-slavery treaties were signed with over fifty African rulers.

***

One country where the slave trade remained particularly rife was Dahomey. A kingdom now located within the present-day boundaries of Benin in West Africa, about 180 miles from east to west, it existed from about 1600 until 1894. In the latter year, the last King of the country, Behanzin, was defeated in two short wars against the French, and the name of Dahomey disappeared from the map when the territory was subsequently incorporated into the growing colonial territory of French West Africa.

It was here on the coast, in October 1849, that HMS *Bonetta* dropped anchor. A three-gun brigantine, or two-masted ship, originally launched in 1836, she was under the captaincy of Lieutenant-Commander Frederick Edwyn Forbes. Having seen some of the horrors of the slave trade and the degrading effect it had on its victims in Africa and South America, he was in charge of a mission to help in putting it to an end for once and for all. His task was fraught with danger, particularly because of the health risks involved. Throughout the nineteenth century, there was a remarkably high mortality rate among Europeans sent there on military or naval service, on account of the tropical diseases prevalent. Among the victims, in the final years of Queen Victoria's reign, were one of her sons-in-law and a grandson. All the same, it was a cause dear to Forbes' heart, and he was determined to make it succeed.

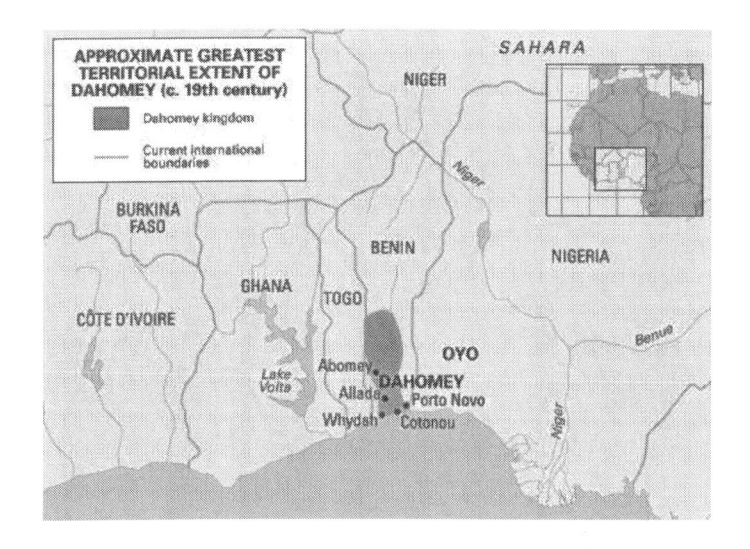

The Dahomans still played a major role in continuing the outlawed practice of slavery, and the British government had for some years been putting significant pressure on them to help bring it to an end. Henry John Temple, Lord Palmerston, who served as Secretary of State for Foreign Affairs from 1846 to 1851 and would end his political career as Prime Minister, was as passionate as the rest of his government colleagues in his detestation of the practice. In one parliamentary debate, he opined that 'it is impossible that this House can too often or too strongly express its opinions in condemnation of the continuance of this abominable traffic'.[1] Yet despite this he was quick to reject any suggestions that Britain should embark on an imperialist policy in Africa, and was dismissive of an idea put forward to him that they ought to annex Dahomey in order to suppress the slave trade at its source.[2]

King Gezo of Dahomey, whose reign had begun in 1818 when he seized power from his brother in a *coup d'état* with the help of a Brazilian slave trader and ruled for another forty years until his reign was brought to an end probably by assassination, was notorious for his cruelty. As Forbes would write in the opening pages of his forthcoming book about his mission and experiences, although Dahomey had been a military nation for two centuries at least, 'it was not until the usurpation of he present monarch, consequent on the unmilitary character of his deposed brother, that she rose to her present height, as the dreaded oppressor of neighbouring nations.'[3]

The slave trade in West Africa had broken down much of the old order of society, and the tribal leaders who were successful and ruthless enough to set themselves up as kings regarded all outsiders as a threat to their influence and way of life. Any illusions that Forbes may have had about the monarch's fearsome reputation were dispelled as he approached the palace of Dange-lah-cordeh, where he was summoned in June 1850. In his account of the mission, he recorded grimly that the walls of the building were 'surmounted, at a distance of twenty feet, with human skulls, many of which ghastly ornaments time has decayed, and the wind blown down. Happy omen! they are not replaced.'[4] This was all part of the image that the King and his people were keen to project to the outside world as a symbol of strength and power.

Before he was allowed to meet Gezo face to face, Forbes and his fellow members of the British had to follow various formalities and rituals, such as passing before the throne, bowing, prostrating and making their obeisance several times. As the Dahoman ministers came to meet then, he observed that the numbers of those in his party were being counted in the event of any physical confrontation and display of force. In the event, everything passed off peacefully, with Forbes, his party and the Dahomans exchanging gifts.

Well aware that his guest represented the most powerful navy in the world, King Gezo was keen to gain his respect, and Forbes and the others were allowed to make themselves comfortable on seats arranged on a high platform facing a courtyard. As part of the ceremony of welcome a party of several hundred African warriors, male and female, paraded in front of the British naval group, as they recited the accomplishments of their leader. This display of warriors and skulls was intended partly to impress the English, and partly as the prelude to an important Dahoman ceremony, the ritual known as *Ek-onee-noo-ah-toh*, or human sacrifice.

At last King Gezo appeared on the platform, accompanied by his Amazon bodyguards. He and Forbes greeted each other cordially. Once the opening exchanges had been concluded, Forbes spoke to him frankly about his severe displeasure with the slave trade. As it would not do to antagonise the guest who represented a power that was on a level with his own, as well as a potential source of revenue to his kingdom, the King listened carefully.

In his reply, he declared that he was 'the first of the blacks,' as Forbes' Queen was 'the first of the whites', and that he did just as he wished. All that Forbes had to offer was a way in which the British could improving the national economy without involving the slave trade. The solution, he advised, was for Dahomey to increase the production of palm oil. If the country was prepared to join the others that had agreed to and signed treaties abandoning the slave trade altogether, the British would undertake to purchase a large quantity of such a commodity that would offset revenues lost to the exchequer through cessation of slavery.

This was not good enough for King Gezo or the Dahomians, to whom the slave trade meant far more than the revenue it provided. The Europeans who intended to buy human beings for labour also provided them with armaments and various European goods, that not only enriched the Dahomans but also gave them crucial power over their enemies. It would never do for the King to give it all up in order to become a peaceful trader in palm oil, he explained, as if he did so he would be much less powerful than the rulers of other African kingdoms in the area, all of which would take it as a sign of weakness. There might be rich financial rewards in trading, but at the risk of forfeiting too much power. On the other hand, there were those who believed that everyone had his price, King Gezo included. A correspondent in *The Times* had noted earlier that year, with some irony, that

> Our best friend in Africa is a certain King of Dahomey, who loves us [the English] so well that he will do anything for us but put an end to the slave trade in his dominions, unless upon the terms of our buying off his royal interest in the traffic by a subsidy of £8,000 a year.[5]

But Forbes was annoyed by his obstinacy and refusal to listen to reason, or what to him seemed like commonsense. Ever since joining the navy as a boy of fourteen, he had seen at close range the misery that the slave trade had caused, and had taken a part in personally rescuing many Africans and setting them free from the cruel fate that would otherwise have beckoned. As his talks with the King continued, so did the rituals of the Dahomans, with warriors firing their long rifles into the air, swinging their weapons overhead, dancing and beating their drums. Forbes began to count the number of warriors under the King's command, and he suspected that he was putting on a major display with the sole intention of trying to make the size and strength of his army seem greater than it really was in terms of numbers, by ordering his men to circle several times in front of the British soldiers. He suspected that his mission was doomed to failure all through the obstinacy of one omnipotent over-powerful man lacking in the normal virtues of human decency and compassion, hellbent on retaining his status as one of the mightiest of African leaders who only wanted to impress other powers without making any concessions.

There were other motives behind his parading of soldiers and the brutality that he seemed to delight in showing to Forbes. It had long been the practice of the British in Africa to negotiate from a position of strength. While they would readily make peaceful treaties when it served their interests, they would use force when it seemed the best method of achieving their objectives.

In April 1847 King Gezo had been persuaded to sign a treaty of friendship and commerce with Britain, but it had not resulted in successful British negotiations for ending the slave trade. He was aware that a British force, including HMS *Bonetta*, had been responsible for attacking and destroying the slave pens at Gallinas in February 1849, a few months previously. Lord Palmerston made it clear in a letter to John Beecroft, recently appointed British consul to the Bights of Benin and Biafra by the British, that he was prepared if necessary to sanction military action against Gezo, who felt impelled to make a demonstration of power to the British group.

They were just about to come and watch, or rather be forced to watch, a particularly chilling ceremony. King

Gezo called them from their seats at the further end of the platform, asking if they wanted to witness the sacrifice. With sheer horror they declined as diplomatically as possible, and begged to be allowed to save at least some of the men. After some conversation with his courtiers, seeing him wavering, Forbes offered him a hundred dollars each for the first and last of the ten. At the same time, Beecroft made a similar offer for the first of the four, which was accepted. Three men were immediately unlashed from their precarious position, but even so they were still forced to remain spectators of the sacrifice of those who had been less fortunate than them.

The King insisted that they had to view the place of sacrifice. Immediately under the royal stand, within the brake of acacia bushes, were about eight men, some armed with clubs, others with scimitars, grinning horribly. When the British party came forward with the greatest reluctance, the mob yelled fearfully, and called upon the King to 'feed them, they were hungry.' Utterly 'disgusted beyond the powers of description,'[6] Forbes and the British party retired to their seats.

As they did so, suddenly they were all startled by the sound of a piercing scream. The men in Forbes's party looked around, and saw a group of Dahomans waving their guns in evident delight. The Lieutenant-Commander asked what was happening, and with the aid of an interpreter, he learned that the people he saw being carried tightly bound hand and foot in small baskets high above the heads of their bearers, while the Dahomans mocked them and prodded them mercilessly with spears and knives as they were passed through the ranks. They were about to be put to death in a ceremony known as the 'watering of the graves'. Each of the victims was dressed in simple white garments, in preparation for being sacrificed, after which their blood would be smeared on the graves of important Dahomans. This, they said, was their national way of honouring their ancestors. Some of those who were about to die had been kept in captivity for more than two years in preparation for this very moment.

Although he had seen some grotesque practices in his time, and throughout all his years of having fought the slave trade, nothing had prepared Forbes for the sheer horror of what he was about to be made to watch. He had never seen such a cruel and bloody ritual. A man was dragged to a pit, the basket carrying him was tipped over and he was thrown down. As his body hit the ground, he was attacked and his head sliced off. At once Forbes entreated King Gezo to stop this barbaric slaughter, but was nonchalantly dismissed with a wave of the hand.

The horror of this occasion never left the Englishman's memory, and in his account he made his abhorrence clear.

> There was not even the poor excuse that these men had committed a crime, or even borne arms against the Dahomans. No; they were murdered, innocent men, at least as far as their barbarous tyrant knew; and if not, may God forgive them in the world to come! ... Murder must work its own suppression; and a nation that practises such foul deeds will, it is to be hoped, soon be forced to mend its ways and change its customs.[7]

The national ritual of watering the graves of their ancestors was a long-established one, the interpreters explained, and nobody had the power to stop it without bringing dishonour to the people of Dahomey. Even the King himself said that he was unable to do so, even if he really wanted to, because he could not go against tradition. 'Gezo, we are assured, has no delight in human sacrifices,' Forbes observed with cutting irony, 'and continues these awful scenes solely out of deference to ancient national customs.'[8]

The procession of Ek-onee-noo-ah-toh, *or human sacrifice, entailing a display of the King of Dahomey's wealth, followed by ritual slaughter*

Gezo, King of Dahomey 1818-58, who made a gift of Sarah to Queen Victoria after he was persuaded by Lieutenant-Commander Forbes to spare her from the ritual slaughter

Sarah Forbes Bonetta as a child in Africa, c.1849, from an engraving based on a watercolour by Octavius Oakley

*Sarah Forbes Bonetta, shortly before she sailed
for England for the first time, c.1849*

CHAPTER 2
Sarah in England

At this point in the proceedings, Forbes caught sight of a small girl. She was a member of the Yoruba tribe, who had been orphaned in 1848 at the age of about five when her family and many other people were massacred by Dahoman slave raiders. Because of her exalted birth, the Dahomans had decided not to sell her to the slave traders, and instead they presented her to King Gezo. He kept her as a royal captive, one of many unfortunate souls destined to be offered before long as a human sacrifice.

The drums were ominously beating ever louder as they brought her towards the pit, and the warrior carried her with ease over his shoulders. Even Forbes, for all his witnessing of the nastier elements of slave trafficking in the earlier days of his naval career, could hardly envisage that a King could wantonly put a small child to death in such a way or for such a reason. Of all the helpless innocent victims that were being butchered, she was surely the most helpless and innocent of all.

But King Gezo evidently had no qualms in sacrificing her as he had all the others. It was explained to Forbes that she had to be put to death as she was an Egbado, an enemy of the Dahomans. The tribal markings on her face showed that she had royal blood, and this blood on the graves of the King's ancestors would be an honour to them. He continued to protest that the girl must not be killed, but the small group of British sailors could hardly force the King's soldiers to change the habit of a lifetime and desist from their barbarous activities. His mission had been to end the slave trade by peaceful means and negotiation, and not to fight or declare war against the Dahomans. All he could do was appeal to King Gezo, telling him that Queen Victoria would never kill a child and would certainly not respect him if he was to do such a thing.

The King appreciated that it was important for him to be respected as a great leader, and not only by his fellow African leaders but also by the Europeans. The little girl had been kept as a captive for two years. While he professed himself powerless to put a stop to the practice that required her as a human sacrifice, he also understood that it would be as well if he did not do anything to provoke the powerful British. After speaking to his ministers, he announced that the killing of the adults would continue as before. However he would spare the girl, who would be given to Forbes's Queen, as a present from the King of the Blacks to the Queen of the Whites.

When the girl was brought before Forbes she was shaking in sheer terror. Having seen so many of her own race savagely killed in these rituals, she was sure that she was about to suffer the same fate. She was still dressed in the white shift that had been put on her in readiness for the final moment. Aware that she spoke Yoruba, and told her though an interpreter that she would not come to any harm. However, she had been given similar reassurances by King Gezo, and at first she saw no reason to believe the white man any more than the man whose forces had taken her captive. Knowing that he would probably begin to gain her confidence if he treated her with gentleness, he lifted her chin and took a careful look at the tribal marks on her cheeks. They consisted of lines that had been cut into her face while she was an infant, confirming that she was an African princess. They had saved her from a life of slavery, but had not prevented her from being brought to the court of her enemies and to almost certain execution.

Through diplomacy, and a measure of sheer good luck, he had succeeded in rescuing her. What he had managed to accomplish was nothing short of a small miracle. When he and his party left the palace, she came with them on their journey from Abomey, the capital of Dahomey. It was almost sixty miles across through rough tracks and countryside from the sea where HMS *Bonetta* had been anchored. Once they had arrived, Forbes took the girl aboard and they sailed down the coast to Badagry.

***

Aina was the name given at birth to the girl who would be known in history as Sarah Forbes Bonetta. She was a West African girl from the Yoruba tribe who lived in south-west and north-central Nigeria, was probably born in 1843 – the precise date is uncertain – at the village of Okeadon.

The Yoruba people were more emancipated than most other African ethnic groups in that the men worked in the fields while the women worked in trade or education, thus giving them financial independence, freedom to travel and even to divorce. Sarah's Yoruba name was 'Aina', meaning difficult birth. It was a name that had often been given to children who had been born with the umbilical cord around her neck.

In 1848 her village was raided by an army from neighbouring Dahomey. Her parents and presumably any siblings were killed during the attack, and she was captured. She could remember very little about the raid, and had evidently blotted it from her memory. All she knew for certain was that her parents had been killed, and she had no idea what had become of her brothers and sisters, but imagined they must have perished as well. Most of what she had been through had been so terrible that she had merely shut it out of her mind.

The Church Missionary Society, an organisation of missionaries from the Church of England founded in 1799, had been based in West Africa for some years, bringing their religious teachings to the people. Forbes brought the girl to them at first, and when members of the Society asked what he was going to do with her, he said he planned to take her back to England with them, as she had officially been given to the Queen. They decided that she ought to be baptised, and a ceremony was accordingly arranged at the mission church at Badagry. When he was asked what name she should be given, Forbes gave her the name of Sarah Forbes Bonetta. Afterwards the missionaries at Badagry dressed her in English clothes, and the wife of the Reverend Vidal painted a watercolour portrait of her.

HMS *Bonetta*'s tour of duty was over and ready to sail back to England. As a warship, she was not designed to accommodate a little girl, but the sailors arranged suitable accommodation for her on board and spent some of their free time on the voyage home keeping her amused. They were friendly enough and Sarah, or Sally, as they began to call her, gradually became less afraid as she realised she was with friends who meant no harm. Her education began as they started to teach her English, and they were very impressed with the speed at which she was able to learn the new language.

Nevertheless, on the journey she stayed as close to Forbes as she reasonably could. He was delighted to have her around him and he spent as much time with her as he was able. She was still dressed in the clothes that had been provided by the missionaries. Never before had she seen such garments as the English were wearing, or been given such food to eat as they were now serving before her.

Despite all the dreadful things that had happened to her recently, she still seemed to maintain a quiet strength. Sometimes Forbes would hear her gently singing to herself, and he wondered whether the songs were ones that she had learned among her own people or else made up herself. As yet, he was not certain what he would do with her once they were back in England. However, he had probably realised that for him and his wife, Mary to adopt her and give her a home at Winkfield Place, Windsor, not far from the castle, with the four young children of their own, would be the most likely solution.

***

At the end of July 1850 the *Bonetta* arrived at Gravesend. Forbes took Sarah home, and from there he wrote a detailed report of his mission to Africa, describing in full his meeting with King Gezo, the rescuing of Sarah and the King's offer of her to Queen Victoria, as if the right to present one human being to another as a gift to another was normal practice. As slavery had now been outlawed throughout the British Empire, she did not belong to anyone as she might have done in an earlier age.

Initially he was reluctant even to consider that the Queen of England would take much notice of the girl. Nevertheless, whatever his personal views on the matter, protocol had to be observed. But although he despised King Gezo, he was still an African King who was sending a present to Queen Victoria, no matter how unusual.

To the Secretary of the Admiralty, he wrote a short formal note about Sarah, as much to make him aware of her presence as anything.

> As a Government Officer I feel myself in duty bound to request their Lordships to lay the offer before Her Majesty, if they should approve thereof.
>
> She now passes by the name of 'Sarah Bonetta' and is an intelligent, good tempered (I need hardly add Black) girl, about six or seven years of age.[1]

The first mention of her in the Queen's journal, and presumably their first meeting, was on 9 November 1850 at Windsor Castle.

Aged thirty-one (six weeks younger than Captain Forbes), Queen Victoria had already been on the throne for eleven years and was the mother of seven children, with two more still to follow. She was extremely impressed to find out that Sarah had mastered the English language so well in such a short time. With a poise and maturity that belied her tender years, the young girl told her as much of her story as she could. After she had been captured, she said, she was brought before King Gezo, who had examined her face and the scars, assured her that she would not be harmed, but then the captors who were responsible for keeping her alive until her execution told her differently. They had confined her in a small space, and for weeks on end she never saw another human being, with only bowls of food pushed through an opening in the wall for her. On some occasions she was forced to witness the other victims as they were dragged out to be sacrificed, knowing that one day it would surely be her turn to die.

The Queen had already heard from Forbes how Sarah was known to be a princess by the tribal marks on her face, an important part of her Egbado identity. Even before it was officially the custom for Egbado children to receive the scars that told the world who they were, young girls would put such marks on their faces themselves, using dyes.

Afterwards she wrote in her journal:

When we came home, found Albert still there, waiting for Capt: Forbes & a poor little Negro girl, whom he brought back from the King of Dahomé, her Parents & all her relatives having been sacrificed. Capt: Forbes saved her life, by asking for her as a present. She was brought into the Corridor. She is 7 years old, sharp & intelligent, & speaks English. She was dressed as any other girl. When her bonnet was taken off, her little black woolly head & big earrings gave her the true negro type. She has been called Sally, after the ship in which she came over.[2]

Queen Victoria had been an only child, and had lost her father, the Duke of Kent, fourth son of King George III, when she was only eight months old. She never had any regular playmates apart from Victoire Conroy, daughter of her *bête noire* John Conroy, her widowed mother's ambitious, scheming comptroller whom she had distrusted and hated so much. Her own formative years had therefore been very lonely. She must have immediately felt a strong bond of sympathy with this orphan child, whose brutal experiences in her short life had been far worse than anything she had ever seen.

After Sarah's visit had come to an end, the Queen wanted her to have her picture taken, and arranged for her to go to the studio of John Jabez Mayall, who had established himself in London as one of the first professional photographers. When she was taken into his premises she had no idea what he was intending to do, and at first when she saw all this unfamiliar equipment, she was quite frightened of of him. When she saw a portrait on his wall of a man wearing a sword, her fear turned to panic. To her, any reminder of a sword could only mean one thing. Mayall and the attendants had to calm her down and assure her that no harm would come to her.

***

There was probably never any likelihood that Sarah would be adopted by the Queen in order to be brought up as one of the still-growing family of Queen Victoria and Prince Albert. Assuming that she was born in 1843, she was the same age as Princess Alice, the third of the children. At this time there were seven princes and princesses in the nursery, the youngest, Arthur, having been born in May 1850, and with two more to follow, Leopold in 1853 and Beatrice in 1857. The thought might have occurred to them, but only very briefly. The royal parents and household between them would readily have appreciated how out of place she would feel if she was brought up as one of them, and the obvious choice was for her to live with another family.

The ideal solution to the matter of her new home to be with her saviour, Captain Forbes, his wife and four young children at Gillingham, and they gladly agreed to raise her as one of their own. The Queen undertook to pay all of her expenses, in addition to taking a great personal interest in her upbringing.

She also asked Charles Phipps, her Keeper of the Privy Purse and Treasurer to Prince Albert, to make all the necessary arrangements. Phipps was a former army officer who had reached the rank of captain.

After accompanying his brother, who was appointed Governor of Jamaica and then Lord Lieutenant of Ireland, as secretary and steward, he became a member of the royal household for about four years, initially as Equerry in Ordinary to the Queen and Private Secretary to Prince Albert. His wife Margaret generally supervised day-to-day affairs in the royal palaces which related to the Queen's domestic affairs. To her would fall much of the responsibility for the care of Sarah, and ensuring that all was well with her and the Forbes family. Charles and Margaret Phipps had several children of their own, the eldest being of a similar age to Sarah.

Over the next few years Sarah was a regular and always welcome visitor to Windsor, and she got on very well with the royal children. Two months later the Queen noted that:

After luncheon Sally Bonita [sic], the little African girl came with Mrs Phipps, & showed me some of her work. This is the 4th time I have seen the poor child, who is really an intelligent little thing.[3]

Forbes also kept a journal, which would form the basis of a two-volume book he was planning to write about his mission to Dahomey. In this he wrote a detailed account of his rescuing the girl whom he was destined to know all too briefly.

I have only to add a few particulars about my extraordinary present The African child. In a former portion of this journal I have mentioned the Okeadon war; one of the captives of this dreadful slave-hunt was this interesting girl. It is usual to reserve the best born for the high behest of royalty and the immolation on the tombs of the diseased nobility. For one of these ends she had been detained at court for two years: proving, by her not having been sold to slave dealer, that she was of a good family.

So extraordinary a present would have been at least burden, had I not the conviction that, in consideration of the nature of the service I had performed, the government would consider her as the property of the crown. To refuse, would have been to have signed her death warrant which, probably, would have been carried into execution forthwith.

Immediately on arriving I applied through the Secretary of the Admiralty, and received for answer that Her Majesty was graciously pleased to arrange for the education and subsequent fate of the child. God grant she may be taught to consider that her duty leads her to rescue those who have not had the advantages of education from the mysterious ways of their ancestors! Of her own history she was only a confused idea. Her parents were decapitated; her brother and sisters she knows not what their fate might have been. For her age supposed to be eight years. She is a perfect genius; she now speaks English well, and has a great talent for music. She has won the affections, with but few exceptions, of all who have known her, she is far in advance of any white child of her age, in aptness of learning, and strength of mind and affection.[4]

***

The Queen had been very impressed by the young princess's exceptional intelligence and natural regal manner. It was clear that she was proving to be a very adaptable young child, having already demonstrated that she could learn to speak good English quickly. Before long she would also show a natural bent for academic studies, literature, art and music. There was no question of sending her away to school, and she was educated privately at the Forbes family home.

After the horrors of having seen her village raided, and family and friends sacrificed to the gods of a conquering tribe, she adjusted well to life in her adopted country. However, it is unlikely that she saw any other Africans whenever she visited Windsor or while she was at her new home in Kent. While there were others who came to London on board ship and were employed at the docks, as well as students and labourers in the large cities, she probably never had any acquaintance with them.

As she was a regular visitor to Windsor Castle and Buckingham Palace, she was taught how to curtsy properly and address the Queen. She learned to wear the clothes that Mrs Forbes made specially, and was also provided with dresses given to her by friends of the family. Naturally her meetings with the Queen were always planned in advance, and on the appointed days she was woken early in the morning to allow for sufficient time to wash and attend family prayers. Every day she ate breakfast with the other Forbes children, and it was brought to the table by a serving girl. Her clothes, which would have been chosen several days previously, were laid out so she could be carefully dressed by Mrs Forbes. From the house they would then take an early carriage ride to Windsor, with Forbes doubtless reminding Sarah gently to be polite, to speak only when spoken to, and always to agree with whatever Her Majesty might say to her. When they arrived at the castle or palace, she was sent to Mrs Phipps, who inspected her to make sure she was presentable to the Queen.

Everything was organised on a very formal basis, with nothing left to chance. Every time she visited, she would see the other royal children as well.

Although Sarah had much to be grateful for in her new life in England, the upheaval of sudden change did not come without some cost. During her first winter in England, she began to suffer from coughs and colds. It was arranged for her to undergo a thorough examination by the Queen's physician, Dr Brown. He listened to her coughing, and concluded that the trouble was not just a respiratory problem but also partly due to stress. To alleviate the difficulty he prescribed various remedies to be taken, but she failed to respond.

The Queen was sure that the cold English winter was taking its toll on her delicate health. If the weather in her new home was really that unsuitable for her, or even harmful, she thought, perhaps it would be better for her if she was allowed to return to her homeland.

Queen Victoria and Prince Albert, 1854

*Sir Charles Phipps, Keeper of the Privy Purse
and Treasurer to Prince Albert, c.1860*

CHAPTER 3

Sarah returns to Africa

Later in January 1851, Charles Phipps wrote to the Reverend Henry Venn about Sarah's future. An Anglican clergyman recognised as one of the foremost Protestant missions strategists of the nineteenth century, and an outstanding administrator, Venn served tirelessly as honorary secretary of the Church Missionary Society in Sierra Leone from 1841 until his death in 1873. Earlier in his career he had been an indefatigable campaigner who regularly lobbied Parliament on the social issues of his day, particularly on ensuring the total eradication of the Atlantic slave trade through retaining the West African Squadron of the Royal Navy. During his work for the society he greatly increased the numbers of European and local clergy appointed in the region, helped to develop trade in African products, and arranged for young Africans to be sent to England for education in business matters in order that they could return to Sierra Leone and put their knowledge to good use for the prosperity of the country.

Phipps informed him that the Queen had at present under her protection a little African girl, had made some enquiries and had been told that the British climate was 'often fatally, hurtful to the health of African children'. Because of this, she was anxious that the child should be educated in one of Her Majesty's dependencies on the African coast.[1]

The belief that Sarah's health would be seriously harmed if she remained in a colder climate was a misapprehension typical of general belief in England in the nineteenth century. Most Africans who had come to Britain had no significant difficulty in adapting themselves to the colder, wetter weather. The slave trade had taken people of African ancestry to Great Britain, North and South America, and the Caribbean, and they had withstood the various climates with no problems. However, once the Queen had made such a decision, she generally got her own way. Forbes had just returned to sea, leaving Sarah with his wife and children in England. He was on his way back to Africa, his determination to help stamp out the slave trade for once and for all redoubled. She was just beginning to feel comfortable in England, and maybe the shock of her having to leave the country again was lessened by her knowledge that Forbes, the man who had become such a father figure to her, would also be in Africa.

Having proved that she was strong enough to survive the raid on her village, the long journey to Dahomey, the months of captivity, an even longer journey back to England and the unsettling transition to a new life in another continent. Now she would have to make the long journey back to Africa where she might face an uncertain, unsettled future.

Sierra Leone had been chosen as her destination. A small country on the coast of West Africa, well to the west of Dahomey, it had been established in the late eighteenth century as a place where Africans who had once been enslaved in England and the British colonies could rebuild their lives, and soon developed as the educational centre of British West Africa. Missionaries had been building churches in Freetown, the capital, and other nearby towns in order to bring their Christian teachings to the area. Among the religious groups who had built missions there was the Church Missionary Society, which helped the British to establish Fourah Bay College in 1827 as an Anglican missionary school with support from Charles MacCarthy, governor of Sierra Leone. It was the first European-style university in West Africa, and remained for some years the only such institution. Forbes had sought the help of the Church Missionary Society after he had initially rescued Sarah, and now it was to one of their schools that she was being sent on the advice of Queen Victoria.

Mrs Forbes had readily taken to Sarah as much as her husband did. Both of them regarded them as their own daughter, and she was thoroughly saddened by the decision to remove her from her care. Nevertheless it was the Queen's express wish that the young girl must return to Africa. With the help of the Queen and Mrs Phipps, Mrs Forbes arranged a suitable wardrobe for her to take to Africa. She also tried to comfort her by telling her that she would probably soon forget them, but added that from time to time, she could return to England and stay with them as long as she wished.

The book that Forbes had been writing about his mission to Dahomey – and the little girl's rescue - was now finished and sent to the publisher. Sarah had been told that it would contain a portrait of her, as well as her story.

He had completed his work on the book, and indeed part of his mission, just in time, for the preparations for her departure were followed by unexpected sad news. During the spring, the family learned that while he was on his way back to Africa to continue his good work, he had been taken ill with the fever, probably malaria, that all too few Englishmen who went to serve in Africa managed to avoid. He died on 25 March 1851, within ten days of what would have been his thirty-second birthday, and was given a burial at sea. His wife and children, and in particular Sarah, were devastated at losing him. She was particularly crushed that her saviour and father figure should have been taken away from her so suddenly, and she was denied the chance to pay her last respects to him.

Had he lived for another year or so, he would have seen some of his efforts bear fruit. In January 1852 King Gezo was persuaded to sign an agreement with the British government to end the slave trade from his country. Nevertheless, he did not fully implement the provisions of this treaty as he continued to allow slaves to be captured in Dahomey, taken to other ports and then sold into the trade, even though he observed the terms of the contract to some extent by stopping the traffic of slaves through the ports on his coast.

***

It was a tearful Sarah who arrived at Gravesend Docks on 17 May 1851, with Reverend Schmid and his wife chosen to travel with her back to Sierra Leone aboard the steamer *Bathurst*. Schmid, a slight, intense man, was sailing to Africa for the first time, and he had been made well aware of the hazards he might encounter on that continent. The presence of his wife gave him some support and comfort, but he was not at all sure of himself as they waited for the signal to board ship. He knew that a large number of the English missionaries who sailed to Africa died within a year or less, usually as a result of fever, as had Forbes. Not for nothing was Sierra Leone known in Victorian England as 'the white man's grave'. Even so, it was quite an honour for him to be entrusted by Mr Phipps with the task of accompanying Sarah. He had written to thank him, as well as to confirm receipt of a cheque for expenses, and also 'a large present' which he and his wife acknowledged 'as a token of Her Majesty's great kindness with humble gratitude; we have not deserved it, for taking care of Sally is our duty. May the Lord bless the giver.'[2]

As for Sarah, this was yet another sudden, even bewildering change thrust on her that she had to absorb. In the space of less than a year, she had been narrowly saved from certain death, taken from Africa to Europe, visited the Queen and the royal children and been treated as an honoured guest, been introduced into a new home, and had suffered from ill-health and the unexpected loss of her greatest benefactor. Still only eight years old, she was being uprooted again and sent to another country.

As part of her education, she had been taught some basic geography. Her elders thought it was important that she should be able to study the map of the world enough to know where England, Europe and Africa were in relation to each other. Yet it was barely adequate preparation for the fact that she was about to be sent on another long journey into the unknown.

After a voyage of thirty-three days, the *Bathurst* arrived at Freetown on 19 June 1851. It had been a difficult passage for them all, with rough seas and very uncomfortable, cramped accommodation aboard the steamer. After the bustling dockside at Gravesend, the harbour area at the sleepy port of Sierra Leone, with its small fishing vessels and equally small ferries, seemed very different and positively tranquil. British ships were anchored offshore alongside a small fleet of fishing boats and commercial ships. By contrast, every morning the town streets would be packed with women carrying bundles of yams, okra, and cassava on their heads. The smells of cooking food drifted through the streets, and the cries of people selling fish and vegetables punctuated the heavy, humid air. During the rainy season, children walking to the school who were fortunate enough to have shoes to wear had to walk carefully round the puddles to keep them dry. Other natives working or living in Sierra Leone went without shoes.

***

At the Church Missionary Society School, the teachers were keen to welcome the little girl in whom Queen Victoria had taken such a close interest. They had been told much about her by the Reverend Venn, who had written to the school to keep them fully informed about Sarah and her life so far.

Venn was a forceful personality who had sometimes had his differences with members of the Church Missionary Society. Forward-looking, with strong ideas as to how everything should be run, he thought it only right that the missions in Africa should be run by the natives of the country in which they were established. He also maintained that education ought to be made available to young girls as well as boys, as the well-being of the former would be for the ultimate good of the strength of family life. In the years to come, he would have an important influence on Sarah's future development.

The students of the Female Institution, which it had been arranged Sarah was to attend, came mostly from Freetown and the nearby villages. African parents who wanted their girls to take their places in the expanding African world knew that a sound education would give them that opportunity in life. However, for most of the students a fee to attend the school was payable. An African family that wanted to send their child to the institution had to provide the small amount of money necessary, and also give up any advantage they might have had from being able to send the child out to earn even a pittance as a labourer. A few of the children were lucky enough to be able to attend the school free of charge, supported by donations to the Church Missionary Society.

Inevitably there were some cultural differences between the English and their African hosts. Some although not all of the missionaries had a poor opinion of or little respect for the Africans, considered that the native religions were inferior, and in their writings used to refer to black people as savages as a matter of course. Many African women used to wear dresses that covered them from their shoulder to their ankles, and some did not cover the tops of their bodies. The missionaries wanted them to wear European clothing, or at least some form of African dress that conformed with English taste. The young African girls who attended school were made to wear English dresses and bonnets, and were taught English hymns. For these African children, attending the missionary school meant giving up most of their own culture.

There the daughters of well-to-do African businessmen dressed in English style and were educated to be proper English ladies. Sarah, who could tell stories of visits to Windsor Castle and who had been on intimate terms with the royal family, received special treatment. She had her own room in which a photograph of Queen Victoria was hung on the wall, while the rest of the students slept in a large dormitory. The Queen continued to pay all the accounts for her education and send her presents of books and toys.

Miss Sass, the head of the school, personally welcomed Sarah and felt honoured to have her there as one of her pupils. The luggage that Sarah had brought with her from England, which included her clothing and several presents from the Queen, was unloaded and put into a cart to be taken to Miss Sass's house.

Among the girls to whom Sarah was introduced was Abigail Crowther. A little older, she had already been to England with her father, the Reverend Samuel Crowther, who later became the first African bishop of the Niger River region. Most of his peers had never once set foot outside Sierra Leone. A few of the other girls had had similar experiences to Sarah in having been captured in the slave raids and rescued by the British ships that patrolled the African coast.

Crowther's own experiences had been not dissimilar to those of Sarah herself. Born in about 1809 in Osogun, Nigeria, and given the name Ajayi, when he was aged twelve he, his mother, brother and other members of the family were captured and sold to Portuguese slave traders. Before his slave-ship left port, it was boarded by a British royal naval vessel and he was taken to Freetown where he was released, looked after by the Anglican Church Missionary Society, taught English, and converted to Christianity. On being baptised in 1825, he took the name of Samuel Crowther after the vicar of Christ Church, Newgate, London. Becoming interested in languages, in 1826 he was sent to England, attended St Mary's Church, Islington, and the church's school. Returning to Freetown a year later, he became the first student to be enrolled at Fourah Bay College, where studied Latin, Greek and the local language of Temne. After completing his studies he became a teacher at the school. His wife Asano, a schoolmistress, had also been rescued from the Portuguese slave ship that originally brought him to Sierra Leone, and converted to Christianity.

According to missionary records kept by the school, Sarah was clearly a favoured student. Miss Sass became her unofficial guardian, and regularly took her shopping in the markets nearby or on picnics. The teachers all treated Sarah with particular attention, allowing her to dress in the clothing that she had brought from England or anything that made from her from material sent by the Queen, while the other children wore simple dresses that had been made for them by the students or staff.

Sarah could tell them about her visits to Windsor Castle, of having taken tea with the royal children, and about her conversations with Queen Victoria and Prince Albert. She had been to places and seen things that her teachers could only dream about. Throughout her time there she was a model scholar and made good progress with her schoolwork. She had spent a year in England, speaking and writing English, had taken private lessons with the Forbes family, and could already write and read from the text they used, Murray's English Grammar. She was also learning to play the piano, and with her musical ear she had a natural ability for the instrument.

Miss Sass used to write regular reports on Sarah's progress at school and send them to Venn. In turn he duly kept Mr Phipps informed as to how well she was doing at her studies. Sarah eagerly awaited the weekly arrival of the steamer that brought mail from England, bringing her regular letters from Mary Forbes, as well as letters and gifts from Queen Victoria.

The Queen continued to send her presents of games and toys, and children's books, which she read eagerly as ever. However kindly meant, these were perhaps not appropriate, in that the girls in the stories were inevitably white, usually with blonde hair and blue eyes. When Sarah looked in the mirror, she naturally saw the face of a slim black girl with dark eyes and hair. Maybe she thought of Mrs Forbes and her fair colouring, and of Princess Alice, who was so close to Sarah in age.

In addition to the Queen's presents, Mr Phipps was regularly sending money directly to the school to cover all Sarah's expenses. Venn was surprised that new furniture had been purchased for Sarah, and gently made his feelings known when he asked Miss Sass whether the expenditure had been suggested by Her Majesty, Mr Phipps or anybody else. He was unsure about Sarah's status, and wondered whether she was to be treated as royalty, or whether she would always be under the Queen's protection.

As yet very few people in Britain were questioning the class system, with the upper strata headed by royalty, a small middle class which also included merchants, military officers, and some of the clergy, and then a large lower class. Although she was without her own independent means and totally dependent on the bounty of the sovereign, Sarah was being treated as an upper-class English person, un unusual if not unique position for somebody of her time. A listing of her expenses appeared in the Church Missionary Society records. The total for her supplies, sent to her by post, was the equivalent of over five weeks' salary for an average poor family living in England.[3]

Sarah wrote to Her Majesty on a regular basis, and the Queen was said to be pleased with Sarah's progress. It can safely be assumed that these reports were always positive. Whether Sarah was always (or ever) what might be called in the jargon of a latter age an academic high-flier, one can only guess. Yet it was surely inevitable that the teachers were expected to show her special leniency and ensure that she was always given high marks for her work, especially as Her Majesty would have asked searching questions had any such reports not been glowing.

In the autumn of 1851, a few months after his sudden death, Lieutenant-Commander Forbes's two-volume work, *Dahomey and the Dahomans*, was published in

England. In his foreword, he explained that it had been his purpose 'in giving publicity to the following Journals to illustrate the dreadful slave hunts and ravages, the annihilations and exterminations, consequent on this trade and to bring prominently before the British public the sacred service they are rendering their fellow-men in prosecuting their increasing efforts to allay those fearful horrors'.[4] A copy of his work, which included the full story of her rescue and her portrait, was presented to the Female Institution.

From time to time Miss Sass and one of her teaching colleagues, Miss Wilkinson, both of whom had come from England to teach in the mission school, would discuss which of the girls showed promise as potential teachers in the next generation. Their idea of their young charges following them in the same profession and showing the other Africans how to live and read the Bible was a regular preoccupation. Some of the native Africans thought that the real purpose of the school was to turn African girls into models of Christian English girls. The students were encouraged to maintain individual flower gardens, and taught to make and mend clothes designed in the English fashion, both of these being skills that were hardly needed in West Africa. In spite of this instruction, the African girls could never be English girls. Sierra Leone was not England, and the white missionaries rarely considered the black girls their equals,[5] let alone consider that perhaps they should not be giving them the same education as they would normally afford to white girls in their own country.

Since having been rescued in Dahomey, Sarah had learned to speak proper English, and every time visitors came to Miss Sass's house, they would be presented formally to her. Visitors would want to know all about her background and early life, and to understand why the Queen had been so fascinated by her. Being the Queen's protegée, at school she had always been given a privileged position apart from the other girls. Perhaps they also wanted to judge for themselves whether she had really deserved such an honour, or had she just been exceptionally fortunate in being saved from an almost certain horrible end and found herself parachuted into a remarkably gilded position, one which some of her peers might have resented.

Miss Sass may also have felt under pressure to help provide a suitably fitting education for the young girl. While the other girls were learning the fundamentals of reading and writing, Sarah was being taught French, as part of her training for a role in English upper-class society. French had been an international language since the beginning of the seventeenth century, and the language of European courts and diplomacy until superseded by English early in the twentieth century. As such it was considered was considered an essential subject for upper-class girls of the day. Although she would not live long enough to see the time, perhaps it was a prescient choice for some of her contemporaries in view of the future French colonial expansion of West Africa, which towards the last years of the nineteenth century would include annexation of the kingdom of Dahomey.

On 24 May 1852 Sarah was permitted to be hostess for a tea for thirty-three of her schoolmates in honour of the Queen's birthday. The occasion ended appropriately as she led them in singing the National Anthem together.

While life for her was secure enough at the Female Institution, occasionally news from the outside world – or perhaps not outside, so much as in effect next door to her in Sierra Leone – came to disturb her equilibrium a little. At around this time King Gezo was continually attacking Abeokuta, a Yoruba city very near her old village. The Church Missionary Society was making efforts to establish a mission in the city. Samuel Crowther had been there during one of the raids, and afterwards he sent a detailed report to the mission offices, describing King Gezo's attack and the valiant but unsuccessful defence of the beleaguered city.

While Sarah was relieved to be there no longer, it saddened and alarmed her to know that in spite of efforts by the English to end the slave trade there, he was still such a threat. Sierra Leone was uncomfortably close to Dahomey, and there could be no guarantee that he would not try to add to his kingdom's territory by any means fair or foul unless anybody was powerful enough to curb his ambitions by standing up to him and his army. The news of his campaign and assault on Abeokuta was a matter of concern for all of the missionaries, and for her in particular it was bound to bring back appalling memories of the mass brutality she had tried so hard to blot out of her memory. There had been talk about some girls at the school becoming missionaries and going to live and work in Abeokuta and other similar cities. It was clearly something that she hoped neither she nor her fellow students would ever be called upon to face, or in her case face again.

News of such occurrences in the neighbouring state of West Africa reached them from people such as Samuel Crowther and other missionaries who would stop in Sierra Leone for a few days' rest during their lengthy journeys. These eminent visitors to the country were always given a conducted tour of the schools, including the Female Institution, as it was in such establishments that Venn believed the future destiny of the continent was being shaped.

One of these gentlemen was James Davies, a missionary and a businessman who was promoting trade and commerce along the west coast of Africa. Like the others, he was introduced to Sarah when he visited the Female Institution as their star pupil. At the time he was aged about twenty-four. Being one of several visitors, she would not remember him any better than the others, but their paths would later cross again before long.

All reports sent from teachers in the institution, given that they were possibly a little gilded and suggesting what Queen Victoria and Mrs Phipps wanted to hear, suggest that Sarah was an industrious girl who continued to make good progress in school during her four years there. Having learnt English with ease, she did well in her French lessons with Miss Sass. With her good ear for music, she also benefited from her piano and singing lessons. In spite of this, her time at the school as a pupil was about to come to a sudden end.

*The Reverend Henry Venn, secretary of the Church
Missionary Society, Sierra Leone, and one of Sarah's
leading mentors in her formative years*

An African school, c.1850, similar to the establishment where Sarah would have attended and later taught as well

CHAPTER 4
Sarah returns to England

Whether Sarah was particularly happy or unhappy in the African school, there is no way of knowing. All that is certain from the documentary evidence is that once she had been there for four years, the institution received a letter from Buckingham Palace in May 1855. In her report of 29 September, Miss Wilkinson wrote that four months previously she had a letter from Mrs Phipps, requesting her to make immediate arrangements for Sarah to be sent back to England by command of Her Majesty.

The Queen had made up her mind a few months earlier. On 27 February Mrs Phipps had written to her friend Elizabeth Schoen, informing her that Her Majesty did not approve of Sarah being in Africa, although without giving any reason why. One can only speculate how and why this might have come about. Whether Sarah had written to her, pleading unhappiness or feeling out of place, concern at resentment from the others of her position as the favoured, almost adopted daughter of the Great White Queen (for which there was no evidence, but which may well have existed), or possibly concern at being in Sierra Leone, uncomfortably close to the ever-present threat of Dahomey and King Gezo not far away, nobody is to know. The most likely explanation was that for some reason she had become unhappy in Sierra Leone and told the Queen that she wanted to return to England. Since the latter had always believed that Africa would be better for her health, it must have been a very persuasive letter.[1]

Almost at once she began to make her preparations to leave for the long voyage back. Miss Sass helped her to pack, checking the luggage, and making sure that all the presents the Queen had sent Sarah were packed and taken on board. On 23 June she sailed for England by steamship under the care of Reverend E. Dicker, who had taught at the Female Institution, and his wife. A small group of rowers took them to a small boat to the steamer offshore, and from the dockside Miss Sass, Miss Wilkinson, and some of the teachers and students watched their star pupil bravely wave goodbye as she sailed away from Sierra Leone. Aboard the steamer, she had a small cabin that contained a cot, a table, chair, and waste pot. Among the items she took back with her were a Bible, that she read diligently every day on the journey, and her treasured photograph of Queen Victoria.

During her years in Sierra Leone, she had seen British ships bring in Africans caught up in the slave trade, the practice that was taking longer to bring to an end than most people had anticipated. Forbes had been largely responsible for breaking up the slave forts that had once held the captives of the famous ship *La Amistad*. Now twelve years old, no longer just a child, and on board ship herself again, she was presumably glad to be returning to the safety of England and another major new upheaval. It had not yet been decided whether she would go back to live with Mary Forbes and her family in what had been her old home, or be expected to settle with a new family.

***

On their arrival at Gravesend in July, the dockside was packed with people carrying bundles to load on to the ships at anchor, or on to the waiting line of horse-drawn carts. By the time Sarah and the Dickers got into their carriage to go to the Church Missionary Society offices off Waterloo Street, it was late and she was exhausted. It had not only from one continent to another, but from an African culture to an English culture that now seemed more than a lifetime away.

Almost as soon as she arrived, it was made clear that there was to be no return for her to the Forbes household. Now a widow with four small children to care for, Mrs Forbes had moved from Windsor to Scotland where she could see and be near the rest of her relations. Having Sarah to look after again would be more than she could manage, and moreover it would not have done for her to be living such a long distance from court.

She was therefore placed with a new English family living in in Palm Cottage, Gillingham, in Kent. Her new foster father, the Reverend Schoen, was a former African missionary, and his wife Elizabeth, aged thirty-nine, was looking forward to her new duties. She had already discussed her at length with Mrs Phipps, her heart had gone out to her and she had made up her mind that she would be delighted to welcome the girl into her home and family. It only remained for the arrangements to be made and a budget for her upkeep to be drawn up and approved.

Her husband, the Reverend James Schoen, had travelled to Africa at the age of twenty-nine and had undertaken missionary work there from 1832 to 1847. In the company of Samuel Crowther, whose daughter Sarah had known, he had explored the regions around the Niger River. After becoming ill with fever in 1847, he was forced to return home for health reasons. In 1855 England was at war with Russia. The Crimean

War produced many casualties, and Reverend Schoen was the chaplain at Melville Hospital near his home.

The Schoen family lived in Canterbury Road, Gillingham, about an hour's journey by train from London. Their house was situated on top of a hill with very few other homes nearby, and with a view of neighbouring fields for miles around. In 1855, the year that Sarah arrived, there were seven children in the house. Of these, Frederick was the closest in age to Sarah. In addition to the Schoens and their children, the household also consisted of a twenty-three-year-old cook and a sixteen-year-old nursemaid.

Mrs Forbes thought that the Queen had made an excellent choice for Sarah. She wrote to Mrs Schoen that she was 'sure you will take care and not let her be made a show of, which makes girls so conceited. It will be very spoiling for her if the Queen takes too much notice of her.'[2]

The adults entrusted with caring for Sarah all understood perfectly what the special relationship between the young black girl and the Queen meant. Mrs Forbes had been slightly concerned lest Sarah might become conceited or spoiled. A letter from Mrs Phipps to Mrs Schoen shortly after Sarah's return to England suggested that she was about to be asked to resume her visits to the Queen, this time at St James's Palace.

The next informal meeting between them took place in December 1855. This time the sovereign's comments in her journal on the girl on whom she had not set eyes for four years were rather less flattering. 'Saw Sally Forbes, the negro girl, whom I have had educated,' she noted; 'she is immensely grown, & has a nice slim figure, but her face is too frightful.'[3]

Sarah took to her new home without any difficulty. She clearly liked living with the Schoen family, and began to refer to Mrs Schoen and Mrs Phipps as

'Mama', although the general impression was that she bonded more strongly with the former. The home education she received was similar to that given to upper-class English girls of the time. As ever, her bills were paid by the Queen and she continued to enjoy a friendly relationship with the royal children, especially with Princess Alice, with whom she used to correspond on a regular basis. The latter had always had a pronounced empathy with those less fortunate or exalted than herself, and a strong desire to help others. She was instantly at ease with ordinary people, and on Sunday mornings at Windsor she would give her governesses the slip and worship from the Sunday pews, because she enjoyed the experience of having people unknown to her on either side. During the family's summer holidays at Balmoral she would sometimes be found in the cottage of one of the tenants, taking them food and drink or helping out with odd family chores around the house and farm.

***

By the new year of 1856 Sarah had settled comfortably into her new family's daily routine, much of which was naturally based around strict religious observance. As a church minister, most of the Reverend Schoen's time was taken up with church activities, and most of the people with whom the family associated were connected with the Church of England. He was also a scholarly man, and had long specialised in the study of languages. Having studied and become familiar with many African tongues, he wrote and published several books and articles on the subject. The atmosphere in the Schoen household was studious but also lively. All of the children were taught at home, and Sarah continued her education with the elder ones. For the rest of her days she would keep in touch with all of them.

Now aged thirteen and on the verge of adolescence, it became apparent that her health was not good, and she suffered regularly from various minor complaints. Mrs Phipps and Mrs Schoen were instructed to make sure that she was kept supplied with enough warm clothing. The Queen was well-known for being completely impervious to cold, and disliking warm temperatures in the royal palaces and residences, much to the discomfort of many of her family and guests. Fortunately, she was prepared to make an exception for Sarah, and whenever the girl was due to come and visit the notoriously draughty Windsor Castle, she asked for a fire to be provided in her room whenever she was visiting, as well as ensuring beforehand that she should be warmly dressed. One letter from Mrs Phipps to Mrs Schoen mentions sending her 'a handsome dress & a pr. Of sleeves & when she comes to London I will give her a scarf edged with white fringe & then if we give her a pink bonnet I think she will do, but to keep her warm she had better wear an under garment'.[4]

Sometimes Sarah saw the Queen alone. At least once she was brought to a 'Drawing Room' during which time the Queen would be available to have brief meetings with foreign diplomats, businessmen, and some members of the public. It was a great honour to be allowed to watch these proceedings. These visits to the Queen would often involve an examination of Sarah's 'work', which meant a review of her progress in learning.

Queen Victoria had made it her practice to bring members of other nationalities and races to the palace and often expressed a willingness to treat them as equals, a progressive way of thinking at the time. To her Sarah was a young African girl who, once given the advantage of a good education, would take her place as a worthy contributor to the well-being of the British Empire. Mrs Phipps's letters frequently referred to Sarah's intellectual progress and the Queen's pleasure in her achievements.

As part of her studies in Sierra Leone, Sarah had learned to sew. Now back in England, she put this to good use by making a pair of slippers for Prince Albert. The Queen was so impressed with them that she asked Sarah if she could make a pair for her as well.

The elder members of Queen Victoria's family were growing up as well. In September 1855 her eldest daughter Victoria, Princess Royal, not yet aged fifteen, was betrothed to Prince Frederick William of Prussia, later Emperor Frederick III. After the news was officially announced the following year, Sarah was presented with a framed picture of the Prince. Her relationships with the royal children always remained good, and she was honoured to be among those invited as guests to the Princess Royal's wedding to her Prussian prince at St James's Palace in January 1858. As she attended the ceremony, the thought doubtless crossed her mind that before long it would be time for her to find her own destiny in marriage. Maybe she realised that the Queen and others would have some influence in the matter.

***

By the new year of 1860 Sarah had been living with the Schoen family, who she regarded very much as her own, for four years, and at long last seemed to be enjoying and benefiting from a settled existence. When she was not at their house in Gillingham she spent some of her time visiting friends in London and Windsor. Occasionally she went further afield to Monck Castle, Scotland, where Mary Forbes now lived, and with whom she had always remained in contact. Her regular visits to the Queen continued, and she maintained her close friendship with Princess Alice. The latter, who was considered by contemporaries to be the most emotionally sensitive of her siblings as well as generally the most sympathetic to other people's problems, had been particularly saddened by the departure of her eldest sister Victoria to the court of Berlin after her marriage in January 1858, and Sarah's friendship may have helped in some small way to fill the vacuum. Alice's matrimonial future was now under active consideration, and in the spring of 1861 she would be betrothed to Prince Louis of Hesse and the Rhine, later to become Grand Duke.

Thanks to the other Schoen children, Sarah was beginning to make friends among her own age group. In October 1860 she and Frederick, the eldest of them, went to London by train together, evidently to spend a night or two with the Vicar of Chiddingly, Hurst Green in Sussex. A cheerful letter to his mother, and the woman whom she always addressed in writing as 'Mama', hints at the undoubted enjoyment of two adolescents enjoying themselves on the outing:

> We arrived safely last evening. Mr Vidal met us at the station before Hailsham. We reached the Vicarage at 10 minutes after 7. It was fully 2 hours ride in the train from London Bridge. I have only 10.6 pence from the 2 pounds you gave us before we started. Besides the tickets I used 3 pence for some cakes and 6 pence for visiting cards and 6 pence this morning for stamps. Will you send me some more money please ... I hope Colonel Phipps will not be angry at my travelling expenses.[5]

For the moment, Sarah's life was relatively settled and carefree. It was not destined to remain so for much longer.

Princess Alice, 1856, the nearest to Sarah in age of Queen Victoria's children and the one to whom she was always closest. She later married Louis, Grand Duke of Hesse and the Rhine

Sarah Forbes Bonetta, 1856

CHAPTER 5
Sarah's marriage

By the end of 1860, now in her seventeenth or perhaps even eighteenth year, it was inevitable that soon Sarah's own matrimonial future would begin to concern the Queen. It was around this time that she received a proposal of marriage.

The man who intended to become her husband was Captain James Pinson Labulo Davies, a widower of thirty-two. Born in 1828 in West Africa, he had been educated in a school run by the Church Missionary Society at Sierra Leone. Despite his early training to work as a ship's captain, his interests at first inclined more to missionary work than in the strictly commercial aspects of shipping. Reverend Venn had been very impressed by what he knew of the young man, his character and abilities. He encouraged him to start his own business and to help others as part of his conviction that progress in Africa depended on native Africans developing their own economy, rather than relying on the English.

Davies expanded his business holdings, and was soon employing about a hundred people, while also pursuing his missionary work, in the course of which he had briefly met Sarah at the Female Institution in Sierra Leone while she was a student aged about twelve. Having been introduced to her on that occasion, he had been made aware by the teaching staff of Queen Victoria's interest in her. When they had first met, Sarah was only a child, while Davies was in his twenties and already married.

Now in his early thirties, he had become a successful African merchant-sailor, naval officer, farmer, pioneer industrialist, statesman, and philanthropist. His first wife, Matilda Bonifacio Serrano, a Spanish lady from Havana, had died in February 1860, nine months after their marriage, following a short illness. Soon after her death he moved to Britain for a time. That same year he wrote to Sarah, introducing himself and asking her if she would be interested in becoming his wife.

His letter must have come as a tremendous surprise to her. Princess Alice being one of her closest friends and also her contemporary, it is tempting to wonder whether they ever discussed his proposal between them. There is no indication of how Lady Phipps (her husband had been knighted in 1858) found out about the proposal, but she was apparently one of the first to know, and she brought up the subject to Mrs Schoen in a letter at around this time.

As Sarah's great protector and most valued friend in England, the person who made financial provision for her, saw to her needs, and continually considered her well-being, Queen Victoria was obviously very interested. She had definite views on a woman's place in society, believing that it was their duty to marry and be a help and comfort to their husbands, rather than remain in what some Victorian ladies referred to as 'single blessedness'.

***

Sarah had taken the tentative proposal lightly. She hardly knew Mr Davies, and at the present had no particular interest in getting to know him better.

However, both the Queen and Lady Phipps were interested in the idea of such a marriage, seeing it as a way of 'settling' the girl's future. With regard to the man who had proposed to Sarah, what his future prospects were, and whether he would he make a match that the Queen would find acceptable, the Queen entrusted Sir Charles Phipps with investigating the matter thoroughly.

Phipps pursued the matter with great care. He wrote a detailed letter to Reverend Venn, asking him for details about Davies's qualities, his character, and his finances. Would he be a candidate for marriage to Sarah of whom the Queen would approve?

Sarah had been very comfortable with her life at Palm Cottage with the Schoens, enjoying the company of the scholarly Reverend with his interest in African languages, and his wife, the kindest woman she had ever met. When Phipps received a favourable report from Reverend Venn about James Davies, and had discussed it with the Queen, the question was put directly to Sarah as to whether she would marry Mr Davies. Taken aback, her first reaction was to say no.

The Queen was adamant that she should marry a man from her own race, and thought Davies would be in a good position to support her lifestyle. It might be the chance of a lifetime, and such an eligible suitor might not cross her path ever again. Sarah had other ideas at first. She protested that she did not love him and that she was not ready for marriage. The age difference between them, thirteen years, may also have made her hesitate.

The Queen had known Sarah for most of her life, ever since she had been an inwardly nervous but also a bright child, eager to learn and eager to please. She had seen her grow into a graceful and charming woman, and one who understood that young women wanted to marry for love. But she also appreciated that the role of women was not always an easy one, and that they were not always free to make their own choices. As long as Sarah was content with the Schoens, the Queen felt, she would not be willing to make a decision based on the practical considerations that Her Majesty thought necessary.

The only solution, she decided, perhaps a little hard-heartedly, was to move Sarah from her home and place her with a new foster family. If she was so, even too comfortable while she was living with the Schoen family she would not even consider marriage at all, she would have to go elsewhere. A letter was sent to Mrs Schoen from the palace, telling her that it had been decided Sarah was live with a Miss Welsh, aged sixty-three, a relative of Lady Phipps, and a widowed relative some ten years older. The new home was to be 17 Clifton Hill, in the Montpelier area of the town in Brighton, about fifty miles away. This new home did not seem a very cheerful prospect for the girl. She arrived there in the spring of 1861, hurt and confused by the sudden changes in her life.

Everyone appreciated that Sarah would be better off marrying someone of her own race. This did not cause a problem for Sarah. She would probably have been happier choosing somebody who was nearer her own age than somebody who had been chosen for her by her guardians. However, arranged marriages were very much the custom in England, with princesses – and even princes – and the upper classes having limited choice. For an African girl living in a white country, the opportunity to find a suitable husband would be even more limited still.

***

Sarah's desolation at suddenly being moved to unfamiliar new surroundings in Brighton was more than a reaction to her separation from the Schoens or the pressure on her to consider marriage, even given that as a small girl, the decisions as to where she was to live had always been made for her by others. Throughout her life, there had been very few places that she felt she could genuinely call her home. She certainly never belonged with the Dahomans who had butchered her family and come very close to doing the same with her. On the ship sailing from West Africa to England she had amused the white sailors, but she had never been one of them. Living with the Schoens in Chatham, visiting the Queen, going on pony rides with the royal children, and attending state functions as an African princess far from her own country, she was an honoured and much-loved guest, but again, she had never really been one of them. Now she was being sent away to a strange town to live with the Welsh family, a decision made by others that was almost a kind of exile.

Sophie J. Welsh, the head of the household, was sixty-two years old. Also under the same roof were Barbara Simon, a widow of seventy-three, their nephew William Welsh, and two servants, Eliza Brewer, aged twenty-eight, and her nineteen-year-old sister, Jane Brewer. It was suggested by Lady Phipps that Sarah might become a suitable companion to the older ladies, a suggestion that may have been kindly meant but one which certainly met with no approval from Sarah herself. If this was the idea, she might have felt aggrieved at being used in this way.

Lady Phipps continued to write to Sarah in Brighton. She asked her what she thought about Davies, and assured her that he had done all he could to ensure his credentials were favourable to the Queen. Sarah had naturally given much thought about marriage, but she wanted to love the man she married, to find him tall and handsome and noble, and to be swept off her feet in the best romantic traditions, not to marry someone she hardly knew and did not love. She must have resented being but under pressure in this way, no matter how kindly it was meant.

Mrs Schoen was probably the only person in whom she could readily confide. Her heart went out to Sarah; she sympathised with her and knew how much she hated living in her new home – if it could be called that - with Mrs Welsh. It was to her that Sarah declared in the spring of 1861 that she had been 'in a state of mental misery & indecision' ever since receiving a letter from her the previous day. She had been tempted to sit down and reply the moment the letter arrived, but knew that it was only sensible to take a little time and consider what she ought to do.

> I shall now tell you truly what my thoughts & feelings are, with regard to Mr Davies. You remember perhaps when he proposed a year ago, I said I could never either love or marry him, and I thought it impossible for us to make each other happy. Had I cared for him, age would never have come in the way of my decision. It would be wicked I think, were I to accept him, when there are others that I prefer. It is useless expecting perfection, but at the same time I do not feel that our two dispositions would mix well together. I don't feel a particle of love for him & never have done so, though now it is a year since he last asked me. What am I to do? Please tell me dear Mama & don't say 'decide as you feel.' I have prayed & asked for guidance but it doesn't come, & the feeling of perfect indifference to him returns with greater force. I am quite stupid & don't know what to do, because I know that there are many of my friends who would say accept him, as then you would have a home & protector & not be obliged to stay at Miss Welsh's for an indefinite time. Others would say 'He

is a good man & though you don't care about him now, will soon learn to love him.' That, I believe, I never could do. I know that the generality of people would say he is rich & your marrying him would at once make you independent, and I say 'Am I to barter my peace of mind for money?' No – never![1]

Sarah understood her position very well, but after having finally found some measure of long-sought inner peace with family and friends like the Schoens, she found it difficult to make a clear decision. She was sure she would never find happiness if she was to move away from that peace into the uncertainty of marriage with a man she did not really know, let alone love.

It upset her that those who were responsible for her well-being had attempted to influence her, or at least tried to put pressure on her to make up her mind, had removed her from the security of her existence at Palm Cottage and the Schoens. It hurt her particularly that she could be so easily made to move from pillar to post. At the worst, it was a reminder that she did not really belong anywhere in England and had no home of her own. She wrote in another letter that she would remain with Miss Welsh until she returned to Africa, this being probably the first time she mentioned the continent of her homeland as a place to which she would eventually like to return.

It was evident that she felt extremely isolated in her new surroundings. She was miserable there, missed London and the previous family, and because of the distance, she was unable to visit the royal family so regularly. The house where she now lived was high on a hill, and with her respiratory problems it must have been difficult for her to negotiate the steep steps every time she returned from the church below. There was a sense of bitterness as she described her discomfort in a subsequent (undated) letter to Mrs Schoen:

> I kept my composure very well till I went into my desolate little pig sty alone, & then I had a regular outburst which I tried hard to overcome .... Don't worry yourself at my writing in this way, for I cannot help it. My head would burst I think if I sat thinking about it all. It ached fearfully last night & is playing the same game this morning.[2]

This was undoubtedly the unhappiest period of her life since she had been rescued in Dahomey. The same year, 1861, was to bring profound misery to Queen Victoria as well. On 16 March her mother, the Duchess of Kent, died at seventy-four after a short illness. Although she was bitterly distressed at her own situation, Sarah penned a charming letter of condolence to the bereaved Queen, and referring in passing to her other pressing concerns at the same time while making light of her own sadness, four weeks later.

> I was very grieved indeed to hear of the loss Your Majesty had sustained in the death of the Duchess of Kent and beg to offer my very sincere sympathy. I should have written to Your Majesty before but thought it would be intruding on your grief. I am now with Miss Welsh and hope to be happy here. Though I cannot help feeling very sorry to leave my dear kind friends Mr & Mrs Schoen, with whom I have resided since my return from Africa, I feel indeed very grateful to them for their unremitting kindness to me. I should be very pleased to show my gratitude to them in some way. They are, and have always been, such sincere friends to my poor Country. The state of affairs out there is very distressing to me. I feel

> deeply Your Majesty's kindness to & interest in me, and hope & trust that I shall never prove ungrateful for all that I have received from you.[3]

Lady Phipps advised Mrs Schoen by letter that it would be appropriate for Sarah to ensure she was dressed in mourning clothes next time she paid a visit to the Queen.

Possibly nobody in the family or household, and certainly not Sarah herself, realised at the time that Prince Albert, who had been created Prince Consort four years earlier, was now desperately overworked and also in poor health. By the end of November he was extremely ill, and on 14 December he died at the age of forty-two. This second close family bereavement in nine months completely shattered the Queen, who remained in grief-stricken seclusion for some time. Six days after his death she wrote to her uncle Leopold, King of the Belgians:

> The poor fatherless baby of eight months is now the utterly broken-hearted and crushed widow of forty-two! My life as a happy one is ended! the world is gone for me! If I must live on (and I will do nothing to make me worse than I am), it is henceforth for our poor fatherless children – for my unhappy country ...[4]

***

Much as Sarah sympathised with the Queen, she still felt a personal sense of abandonment. Her life at Brighton did not become any the more cheerful, and she was still miserable living far away from the adopted family whom she had grown to love. Throughout her short life she must have felt deeply that she had never yet found the safety and security of living in a place that she could really call her home. It was inevitable that under such circumstances she began to ponder more deeply what married life with James Davies would mean, and what improvement it would entail on her present unhappy circumstances. At the same time, it led her to consider how life in England might be like for her without the support of the Queen. She could hardly envisage life on her own as an African woman, and she certainly did not wish to contemplate an eternal existence with the elderly Miss Welsh, with whom she had nothing in common.

It was evident that Queen Victoria and Reverend Henry Venn were highly impressed by James Davies and thought him a suitable husband. He had the financial resources to support Sarah, and had promised to treat her well. She had no chance to go out on her own or make friends, particularly in a country that was not her own. If she was to reject him, her opportunities would be severely limited.

Queen Victoria, who some of her family and household feared was in danger of losing her reason through grief, was increasingly self-absorbed. It was a far cry from the situation when Sarah had met her for the first time some eleven years earlier. Her Majesty was now a very different woman, with very little of the empathy and solicitude that she had once shown so freely to the little recently-rescued orphan child from another continent.

As she was still paying for Sarah's upkeep, she may have been tiring of the commitment into which she had entered, and felt it was time that this arrangement should come to an end. Marriage to a suitably well-off gentleman would absolve her of such responsibility. Gradually Sarah began to have second thoughts. Perhaps she accepted that the Queen's judgment was right after all, and arrived at the conclusion that even an arranged marriage – which was by no means unusual for girls at the time - would be a better alternative to her dreary life at Brighton, living with people with whom she had nothing in common, and which was hardly pleasant at best if not quite insupportable at worst. Marriage after all was the ultimate destiny for most women of the time, and she could ask for little more than a kind, supportive and financially secure husband.

In March 1862, she went to Windsor and visited the Queen, no longer the welcoming mother of earlier and more carefree days. She had evidently come to her decision, and told her that she had agreed to become Mrs Davies.

***

The wedding took place at St Nicholas' Church, Brighton, on 14 August 1862, a day of light but steady rain. An article in *The Times*, about half of which was taken up with an extract from Forbes's book containing his description of her, appeared the following day. Under the heading 'Interesting marriage in Brighton', it said the event would

> unite a lady and gentleman of colour, whose previous history gives to the ceremony a peculiar interest, chiefly to those who have been, so long and so deeply interested in the African race, and who have watched the progress of civilization caused by the influence of Christianity on the negro; and the ceremony will also tell our brethren on the other side of the Atlantic that British ladies and gentlemen consider it a pleasure and a privilege to do honour to those of the African race who have proved themselves capable of appreciating the advantages of a liberal education.[5]

It also noted that the Queen had 'provided the whole of the outfit', and that the royal family had all sent presents.

Captain Forbes' brother gave the bride away at the ceremony. None of the royal family were present at the wedding, but nevertheless it was quite a grand occasion. The party that did attend, arriving from West Hill Lodge, Brighton in ten carriages and pairs of greys, was made up of 'White ladies with African gentlemen, and African ladies with White gentlemen', and there were sixteen bridesmaids.

For the young woman at the altar, it must have been a day of very mixed emotions. It was to some extent an arranged marriage, as indeed were many matrimonial unions among the royal family and upper classes in Victorian England. She was marrying a man several years older than her whom she probably felt she could never really love, but at least he seemed to be a good, steady, industrious, hard-working gentleman. Moreover, after such an unsettled life, during most of which she had been part of somebody else's family, and latterly after being little more than a lodger, at least she would have a home of her own. Mrs Schoen, who was the nearest she had had to a mother, had done her very best to console her, and the royal family had tried to make the wedding seem the right thing for her. What other alternative would she have had?

As she entered the church, the young women who had become her friends lined up for the procession. There were many embraces, some tears and a few last-minute adjustments to her gown. From the church interior, the sound of hymns filtered through the heavy wooden doors of the vestry as the ceremony was about to begin.

Sarah had several bridesmaids. Some were African, including the groom's sister and several other young women from the continent who attended schools in

England. They were dressed in white gowns with red trim. The next four bridesmaids were English, also in white gowns but with blue trim. A procession of very young girls followed them. Four English groomsmen accompanied James Davies to the front of the church, and stood while the bridesmaids walked slowly in a procession down the aisle and formed a line across the front of the altar. Sarah's gown was made of white silk with white trimmings, while a wreath of orange blossoms on her head held the white veil in place. By her side, and giving her away, was another Captain Forbes, the brother of her saviour, the man who had given her his name and who would have been so proud to have lived to see the day. The Reverend Venn and Reverend Nichol from the Church Missionary Society assisted with the ceremonies.

After the hymns, the blessing of bride and groom and the exchange of solemn vows of marriage on both sides, Sarah Forbes Bonetta became Sarah Forbes Bonetta Davies. There was a burst of cheering and congratulations and more tears as the newly-married couple left the church. Those who had been unable to find space in the small church and were waiting outside in the rain applauded enthusiastically as Mr and Mrs Davies were ushered into a waiting carriage under a canopy of umbrellas.

A wedding breakfast was held after the ceremony at West Hill Lodge, attended by the Schoen and Forbes families. The celebrations lasted throughout the day, coming to a close at around 4.30 p.m. as the married couple were driven to the station en route for London.

Sarah Forbes Bonetta, 1862

Sarah Forbes Bonetta, 1862

*The wedding of Sarah and James Davies
at Brighton, 14 August 1862*

*St Nicholas Church, Brighton, where the wedding of
Sarah and James took place*

Sarah and James Davies, 1862

Sarah and James Davies, 1862

CHAPTER 6
Mrs Davies in Africa

Whether Sarah would have preferred to stay in England after her marriage, there is no way of knowing. She was given no choice in the life she would be leading with James Davies. However, his work was in Africa, and that was where she belonged. The couple may have lived in Bristol for a short time, but before long they had settled in Freetown, and apart from occasional visits to England they spent most of their married life in Africa. It was here that he would continue his business ventures, and here that she would also find employment, becoming a teacher at the Female Institution.

At the time, the Church Missionary Society's school in Sierra Leone that she had previously attended was involved in a controversy over who should lead the schools and the mission stations. The English women who taught at the Female Institution in Freetown often considered themselves culturally superior to the Africans they were teaching. The class system in England was part of the ideology that the missionaries brought with them, and the English teachers were not prepared to work under the direction of the native peoples. Alienation between the church and the Africans was all too often the result. Reverend Venn was among the far-sighted minority who believed that all of them should work with the African teachers and clergy, and show tolerance and understanding in order to eliminate any divisions.

All of the young African women who were eventually recruited to work as teachers had all been taught by English people. They were expected not only to teach in English but also to pass on the values of the mother country. As she had been Anglicised throughout most of her short life, nineteen-year-old Sarah was in a very different position to that of her contemporaries. She had received an excellent education, had spent much of her young life in England, and knew just as much about English culture as did the British teachers with whom she would be working. With her experiences, she knew far more than they did of upper-class life.

***

Having had such an unsettled life in her early years, Sarah was now the wife of a successful businessman and, for a while, relatively free of financial worries. As somebody who also knew and was liked by Queen Victoria, she was in quite a fortunate position. She taught at the Female Institution at Sierra Leone and at a similar school in Nigeria, and it was only to be expected that some of the teachers were jealous of her status. An intelligent young woman with a good education, she was full of ideas as to what African girls needed to be taught. She set herself and her charges high standards, believing that African women could be at least as effective as their English counterparts. There is nothing to suggest that she was unhappy in her career, but she may have been aware that her English background and the more comfortable times she had known at or close to the English court might engender resentment among some of her colleagues.

At first there was every chance that Sarah would become head of the school that she had once attended. However, within a few months it was confirmed that she was about to become a mother. In 1863 she gave birth to a daughter, and sought permission from Queen Victoria to give her the same name. The Queen was flattered and readily agreed, and even more so when asked to be the girl's godmother.

The baby was christened at a church in the town of Badagry, a former slave port in Nigeria, and the Queen sent a gold cup, salver, knife, fork and spoon, all engraved 'To Victoria Davies from her godmother, Victoria, Queen of Great Britain and Ireland, 1863'.

After her daughter was born, Sarah moved to Lagos. She continued to enjoy a good relationship with the Queen, albeit from a considerable distance. The monarch remained supportive and continued to take in interest in her well-being and that of the family, and she was one of only two people from the city whom the Royal Navy had standing orders to evacuate in the event of an uprising in the capital. The other was Bishop Samuel Crowther, a close associate and friend of Captain Davies. They had collaborated on a couple of social initiatives in the area, one being the opening of The Academy, a social and cultural centre for public enlightenment, in October 1866 with Crowther as the first patron and Davies as president.

***

The young family paid another visit to England in December 1867. Sarah wrote in her diary that she saw the Queen at Windsor Castle on Monday, and perhaps significantly 'Victoria was sent for again on Wednesday'. The Queen gave her little girl a doll and a gold locket with the Queen's picture inside. As ever,

Queen Victoria's own record of the meetings was short and to the point;

> After luncheon saw Sally, now Mrs Davis, & her dear child, far blacker than herself, called Victoria & age 4, a lively intelligent child, with big melancholy eyes.[1]

On the second visit, Sarah was evidently excluded from the company, as the Queen wanted to ask the others some searching questions about how she was getting on. She understood perfectly, and accepted it with good grace, writing to Mrs Schoen the following week about it:

> The conversation was all about Captain D & myself, so out of delicacy I was not asked to go up. They were all Charmed with the child, & the Queen gave her on Monday a dear gold locket with a brilliant (diamond) on it & her likeness inside ... Victoria has just been to have her photo done for the Queen – tis to be coloured. You Cannot think how affected they all were with her, & yesterday Prince Leopold took possession of her & the Queen gave her sweets. No one saw her with Her Majesty yesterday except the Prince and Psses. I hope all are well, I suppose it is terribly cold as usual.[2]

During these years it was apparent that Sarah was happy and settled in her new life as a wife, mother and teacher in Lagos at the Female Institution, undertaking additional work for the Church Missionary Society. Despite the hospitality she had received in England, she had probably never really felt fully at ease there. Back in Africa, and in a peaceful unthreatened existence completely at odds with the horrifying experiences of her early days, she found contentment.

If the marriage had not been a love match at first, it almost certainly ripened into something very like it. Her letters were ample testimony that she had come to grow very fond of James. He continued to work hard, much of the time under the guidance of Reverend Venn, in building up business and commercial schemes in the area. Venn hoped he would be able to recruit the next generation of African leaders who would contribute towards stabilizing West Africa in the unsettled years that had followed the elimination of slavery.

***

Sarah and James had three children altogether. Little Victoria had been followed by a son, Arthur, born in 1871, and a second daughter Stella, in 1873. Like his elder sister, Arthur was educated in England and Europe.

She also paid at least two other visits to Windsor during the 1870s. In March 1873 Queen Victoria noted in her journal that she saw eight-year-old Victoria Davies again, 'wonderfully like her mother, very black, & with fine eyes'.[3]

Two years later, to the week, they came again, as a further entry reveals. 'Saw Sally Davis [sic], her husband & 2 children, all, coal black.'[4]

James Davies became a member of the Legislative Council from 1872 to 1874. In the latter year Lagos Colony was for a time amalgamated into the Gold Coast. It is apparent that he was not particularly successful or fortunate in his business career. In the spring of 1868, Sarah gave an outline of his problems in a letter to Mrs Schoen:

The fact is James is infinitely too good & kind to everybody, & he is not appreciated, & when he does anything, people detract him as a matter of course, & I think it his duty – to labour for the benefit of others but because they are all jealous of his position & influence they are only too ready to cry him down & abuse him, but thank you, that will not hurt him for he knows in whom he has trusted & is safe...[5]

***

When James's business failed, the family suffered significant financial losses. They were probably not severe enough to cause them any significant hardship. Even so, for Sarah, whose short life had already been quite unsettled enough, it would prove one misfortune too many.

Her health had never been good, and perhaps now aggravated by worry and stress, her respiratory problems worsened. Ironically a similar fate had befallen Alice, her closest friend and the nearest to her in age among the royal family, who had succumbed to diphtheria in 1878 at the early age of thirty-five. Sarah became too weak to teach, and developed a hacking persistent cough. When she failed to recover, Davies grew ever more concerned. At length the illness was diagnosed as tuberculosis, and she agreed to go to Funchal, the capital of the Portuguese island of Madeira, for treatment and recuperation, as it was well-known as a suitable place with its mild climate for those with respiratory diseases. She and her younger daughter stayed at the Royal Edinburgh Hotel, where from the window she had a charming view of neatly landscaped jacaranda trees.

At first there was a mild improvement in her health, and in the spring of 1880 she wrote to Mrs Schoen to acknowledge a letter she had just received.

I started for this Island the next Tuesday, & since being here so ill as I was have been obliged to keep quiet; writing which I always liked has become also a task. I nearly died in Lagos this last illness I had in January, & the cough I told you of, seeming rather to increase than otherwise. My poor husband who has had enough trouble to kill two ordinary men, made up his mind at the instigation of the doctor to send me here for some months change & here I am with Stella & her nurse for an indefinite period. The day after tomorrow makes one month since our arrival. I am slowly picking up strength, but the cold winds, which even here is to be felt sometimes, do not improve the cough, still it is much better to what it was in Lagos. The doctor says he will cure me in six months, & you must know, that my lungs are affected besides my throat being sore from the irritation of coughing.

Stella keeps well & seems quite to like Madeira. Is not that fortunate? I think it agrees with her. I have not seen much of the place, as the doctor forbids my walking far or even much driving. There are beautiful mountains all around us & lovely flowers, such excursions one could make here climbing over the mountains to the other side. There are two or three nice family parties in this hotel staying, they are all very pleasant. Last week Mrs Burton from the Female Institution or as it is now termed the 'Annie Walsh Memorial School' arrived on two months sick leave. I never knew her before only her sister who died at Lagos, Mrs Faulkner. I heard from Victoria, it seems she is in England; the climate of that part of France she was at not agreeing with her; whether she will return there or not is uncertain, but she would not return to that school in any case I fancy. Meanwhile she will keep quiet and regain her strength at Mrs Christie's and will be studying at home quietly till her father decides what is to be done. I should like her to perfect the languages German & French & her music. It is only in the two countries one can accomplish this, I know. We have nothing to give her, but a good education which will always make her independent.[6]

Gradually the rest and mild climate had some effect, and she seemed to feel a little better. Within six months, she had decided, she would be cured and ready to resume her old life in Africa once more.

Sadly, it was not to be. Later that summer she had a relapse, gradually became weaker, and the doctors admitted that no more could be done but to make her as comfortable as possible in the remaining time she had left. The girl who had so nearly met a hideous death in her homeland and shared the bloody fate of her family, yet demonstrated a remarkable resilience in the face of tragedy and insecurity since then, had met her last enemy.

Queen Victoria was at Osborne when her family prepared her for the worst. On 23 August, she wrote in her journal, she was 'grieved & shocked to hear, that poor Sally Mrs Davies, was hopelessly ill at Madeira.'[7]

There had been no recovery. News travelled slowly from overseas, and Sarah had died eight days previously. Not for another twenty-four hours did the Queen learn that the disease had already taken its course.

> After luncheon, saw the Judge Advocate, & then saw poor Victoria Davies, my black godchild, now 17 who heard this morning of the death of her dear mother at Madeira. The poor child was dreadfully upset & distressed, & only got the news, as she was starting to come here, so that she could not put off coming.

Her father has failed in business, which aggravated her poor mother's illness. A young brother & a little sister, only 5 were with their mother. Victoria seems a nice girl, very black & with very pronounced negro features. I shall give her an annuity.[8]

Although she was undoubtedly upset by the news, it comes across as a rather matter-of-fact entry, somewhat devoid of feeling. What, one wonders, had happened in the intervening years? Although to suggest she was less caring than she had been as a young woman in her thirties, Queen Victoria had become tougher as a personality in middle age, particularly after the deaths of her mother and husband in quick succession, and always ready to find fault with even her own children to whom she had been so close when they were smaller. She may have resented Sarah's temporary show of defiance before agreeing to marry; she may have just tired of the general responsibility, although her readiness to make provision for her goddaughter, the motherless eldest girl (if not perhaps her siblings as well) is significant. Her willingness to set an allowance aside was ample testimony of her desire to continue helping the family in their time of need and sorrow.

***

Sarah had left instructions that after her death she wanted to be reunited with her rescuer and beloved foster father, Captain Forbes, by being buried at sea as well. This was to be denied her, and she was laid to rest close to where she had ended her days. Her grave was No 206 in the British Cemetery near the Anglican Holy Trinity Church, Rua Quebra Costas Funchal, Madeira. At present it is not marked by a headstone.

She is more conspicuously remembered closer to her married home. Her widower erected a granite obelisk-shaped monument over eight feet high in her memory at Ijon, in Western Lagos. The inscription reads:

IN MEMORY OF PRINCESS SARAH FORBES
BONETTA
WIFE OF THE HON J.P.L. DAVIES WHO
DEPARTED THIS LIFE AT MADEIRA AUGUST
15TH 1880
AGED 37 YEARS

Bishop Samuel Crowther, 1867

Queen Victoria and Princess Beatrice, c.1880

Lagos, c.1900

Funchal, Madeira, where Sarah sought a cure from her tuberculosis in vain, with the English cemetery in the background. Engraving after a painting by Karl Bryullov, c.1850

*The English cemetery at Funchal,
where Sarah was laid to rest*

Afterword

Having become a widower for the second time, nine years later James Davies married once again. His third wife was Catherine Kofoworola Reffle, and their wedding took place in Africa in 1889. Although his earlier business may have failed, he was a man of determination, and it was not long before initiative and business acumen enabled him to prosper before long. Around 1879 and 1880 he pioneered cocoa farming in west Africa after obtaining the seeds from a Brazilian ship and also from the island of Fernando Po, off the west coast of Africa. It led to his establishment of a prosperous cocoa farm in Ijon, and he shared his knowledge of the business as well as a share of his profits to Jacob Kehinda Coker, who used the proceeds from his own cocoa farm to support Christian evangelical interests. Sir Brandford Griffith, who was Chief Justice of the Gold Coast early in the twentieth century, testified to Davies having been the first person to plant cocoa on the mainland.[1] He died on 29 April 1906 at the age of seventy-seven, and was buried in Lagos.

In November 1890 Victoria Matilda, the elder daughter, married John Randle, a Lagos doctor and politician, and the Queen provided her with the material from which her wedding gown was made. Since her mother's death, she had continued to visit Queen Victoria on various occasions. Only one of these, probably the last, was ever reported in the Court Circular. On 2 July 1900 Bishop James Johnson of Lagos escorted her and her children to Windsor Castle, where it was reported that the Queen 'granted the children the favour of kissing her hand, whilst she herself kissed them and their mother also and gave some nice presents to the little ones'. After a little small talk with them, the Queen turned to the Bishop and made 'some anxious inquiries about the present rising in Ashanti land, which seemed to have affected her much, and about the character of the climate at this time (which is a very wet season in West Africa generally) in view of the effect it might have upon her troops, and especially their European officers who are engaged in suppressing the rising.'[2] This referred to the intermittent campaigns in the Gold Coast between the Ashanti empire on one hand, and the British empire and British-allied African states mainly due to Ashanti attempts to establish control over the coastal areas.

Now aged eighty-one, Queen Victoria was ageing fast, and by the end of the year it was recognised that she did not have long to live. She died in January 1901. The royal annuity of £40 that she had granted to Victoria and her family on the death of Sarah twenty years earlier had been put to good use, enabling her goddaughter to be educated at Cheltenham Ladies' College.

John Randle was born on 1 February 1855 in Regent, Sierra Leone, the son of Thomas Randle, a liberated slave from an Oyo village in the west of what later became Nigeria, moved to Lagos and set up a successful haberdashery business. He was educated at the missionary school in the village and then at the Church Mission Society grammar school in Freetown. Becoming a dispenser at the Colonial Hospital in 1874, he moved to Accra where he saved enough to pay for formal medical training at the University of Edinburgh between 1884 and 1888, graduating with a gold medal in *materia medica* and in the process becoming one of the first West Africans to qualify as a doctor in the United Kingdom.

In 1892 he angrily resigned from the Colonial Service. He felt discriminated against that as an African he was receiving only about half the salary of a European colleague with similar training, and at being required to serve as a doctor in places a long distance from Lagos. After persuasion he withdrew his resignation, but only on condition that he was granted an increase in salary to £500 per year. One year later he was dismissed for his persistent refusal to make tours of duty to a British military outpost at Ijebu-Ode, some distance from Lagos, and devoted himself to a successful private medical practice, treating patients from all levels of society, providing free treatment to the poor. In a change of career he subsequently became active in Lagos politics. When the First World War broke out in 1914 he was a vocal supporter of Britain during the First World War, insisting that they should never 'forget the wider principle that we are citizens of the British Empire'. He died in February 1928.

Victoria and John had two children, Beatrice (named after Queen Victoria's youngest daughter) and Romanes Adewale, otherwise known as John. She was one of the Queen's last visitors before the latter died at Osborne on 22 January 1901.

Their marriage did not long survive the birth of their children, of whom she was granted custody. They lived in London from 1898, where she met the composer Samuel Coleridge-Taylor and provided him with a Nigerian theme that he published in a book of African folk songs in 1905. Some years later she moved to Sierra Leone. She died in 1920, probably in Lagos. Dr

Randle died in 1928. Most of the family's descendants now live in either England or Sierra Leone, while a separate branch, the aristocratic Randle family of Lagos, remains prominent in contemporary Nigeria.

***

Not long after the publication of Walter Dean Myers' biography in 1999, Sarah's great-great grandson Arnold Awoonor-Gordon, a retired broadcaster from Sierra Leone who lived at Chatham, wanted to know more of what he had gathered was his highly unusual ancestry. As he commented, it was remarkable for an African slave to be taken on by the British royal family in the 19th century. Although the relationship was more one of friends than adopted family, and even though the Queen and her family did not share they sometimes racist attitudes of nineteenth-century society, it was 'really ahead of its time'. Having decided he ought to research his family history, he contacted Windsor Castle, and was delighted to find that the stories that his family had a direct connection with British royalty were fact and not fiction.

Queen Victoria, he said, was a pioneer at the time, keenly fascinated by other cultures and very open-minded. Above all, 'Captain Forbes essentially saved Sarah's life, rescuing her from years of slavery and even death.' Although it would never have happened without his bold intervention, the Queen was partly responsible, and he saw her as a leading campaigner against the slave trade. He added that he always thought of Queen Victoria as 'someone who helped to rescue my relatives. As Victoria herself described in her diaries, she 'saved her little Sally".'[3]

*Victoria Randle, Sarah's daughter, with her children
Beatrice and Romanes (John), 1901*

Acknowledgements

My particular thanks are naturally due to the late Walter Myers, whose own book was an invaluable major source on the details of Sarah's life; and to my wife Kim, whose sterling work in reading the draft, and discussing as well as making suggestions for improvement, are greatly appreciated as always.

Reference Notes

INTRODUCTION

1 *Daily Mail (Weekend)*, 23 December 2017
2 Connor, *Daily Mirror*, 8 December 2017
3 Magnus, p.171
4 Brown, *Washington Post*, 27 November 2017
5 Thomas, p.172

CHAPTER 1

1 *New York Times,* 10 August 1861
2 Ridley, p.540
3 Forbes, Vol 1, p.7
4 *ibid.*, p.75
5 *The Times*, 8 April 1850
6 Forbes, Vol 2, pp 50-51
7 *ibid.*, Vol 1, p.53
8 *ibid.*, Vol 1, p.32

CHAPTER 2

1 Myers, p.23, Forbes to Sec of Admiralty, 3 August 1850
2 Queen Victoria's Journal, 9 November 1850
3 *ibid.*, 11 January 1851
4 Forbes, Vol 2, pp.206-208

CHAPTER 3

1 Myers, pp.39-40, Phipps to Venn, 25 January 1851
2 *ibid.*, p.45, Schmid to Phipps, 16 May 1851
3 *ibid.*, p.59
4 Forbes, Vol 1, p.4
5 Myers, pp.55-56

CHAPTER 4

1 Myers, p.62
2 *ibid.*, p.71, Mary Forbes to Mrs Schoen, n.d.
3 Queen Victoria's Journal, 9 December 1855
4 Myers, p.77, Mrs Phipps to Mrs Schoen n.d.
5 *ibid.*, pp.91-92, Sarah to Mrs Schoen, 3 October 1860

CHAPTER 5

1 Myers, pp.106-8, Sarah to Mrs Schoen, 16 March 1861
2 *ibid.*, p.110, Sarah to Mrs Schoen, n.d.
3 *ibid.*, p.111, SFB to QV, 12 April 1861
4 *Letters of Queen Victoria, 1837-1861*, Vol 3, p.473, Queen Victoria to King Leopold of the Belgians, 20 December 1861
5 *The Times*, 15 August 1862

CHAPTER 6

1 Queen Victoria's Journal, 9 December 1867
2 Myers, p.127, Sarah to Mrs Schoen, 13 December 1867
3 Queen Victoria's Journal, 29 March 1873
4 *ibid.*, 31 March 1875
5 Myers, p.124-5, Sarah to Mrs Schoen, 22 April 1868
6 *ibid.*, p.133-5, Sarah to Mrs Schoen, 7 April 1880
7 Queen Victoria's Journal, 23 August 1880
8 *ibid.*, 24 August 1880, Osborne

Afterword

1 Elebute, pp.111-119
2 *The Times*, 22 August 1900
3 Connor, *Daily Mirror*, 8 December 2017

Bibliography

Bamgbose, Kemi, 'Sarah Forbes Bonetta: The Yoruba Princess Who Captured Queen Victoria's Heart'. In *New African Woman*, November 2016

Brown, DeNeen L., 'Britain's black queen: Will Meghan Markle really be the first mixed-race royal?' In *Washington Post, 27 November 2017*

Connor, Laura, 'The little-known tale of the African slave girl adopted by Queen Victoria'. In *Daily Mirror*, 8 Dec 2017

Duff, David, *Hessian Tapestry* (London: Frederick Muller, 1967)

Elebute, Adeyemo, *The Life of James Pinson Labulo Davies: A Colossus of Victorian Lagos* (Lagos: Kachifo, 2013)

Forbes, Frederick E., *Dahomey and the Dahomans: Being the journals of two missions to the King of Dahomey, and residence at his capital, in the years 1849 and 1850*, 2 vols (London: Longman, Brown, Green and Longmans, 1851)

Magnus, Philip, *King Edward the Seventh* (London: John Murray, 1964)

Marsh, Jan, *Black Victorians: Black people in British art* (Michigan: University of Michigan, 2009)

Morrison, Shelby, 'An African Princess in Queen Victoria's Court'. In *Royalty Digest* (114), December 2000, pp.184-185

Myers, Walter Dean, *At Her Majesty's Request: An African Princess in Victorian England* (New York: Scholastic Press, 1999)

Queen Victoria's Journal, online

Rappaport, Helen, *Queen Victoria: A Biographical Companion* (Santa-Barbara, CA: ABC-CLIO, 2003)

Ridley, Jasper, *Lord Palmerston* (London: Constable, 1970)

Silvy, Camille, 'The African Princess: Sarah Forbes Bonetta'. Black History website, August 2015 http://www.blackhistorymonth.org.uk/article/section/real-stories/the-african-princess-sarah-forbes-bonetta/

Southern, Kieran, 'How Queen Victoria adopted an African slave girl whose parents were murdered will be revealed in ITV's Christmas special'. In *Daily Mail*, 9 December 2017

Sarah Forbes Bonetta - The African Princess in Brighton Brighton & Hove Black History, https://web.archive.org/web/20030508111257/http://www.black-history.org.uk/bonetta.asp

The Times

Thomas, Nicholas, *Entangled Objects: Exchange, Material Culture, and Colonialism in the Pacific* (Cambridge, Mass.: Harvard University Press, 1991)

Victoria, Queen, *The letters of Queen Victoria: A selection from Her Majesty's correspondence between the years 1837 and 1861,* ed. A.C. Benson & Viscount Esher, 3 vols (London: John Murray, 1907)

Williams, Kate, 'The royals and race: from Victoria and Abdul to Harry and Meghan Markle.' In *The Guardian*, 10 September 2017

Index

Albert, Prince Consort (1819-1861), 8, 37, 38, 39, 53, 67; death, 80
Alfonso III, King of Portugal (1210-1279), 13
Alice, Princess, later Grand Duchess of Hesse and the Rhine (1843-1878), 38, 53; Sarah's friendship with, 65, 68, 73; death, 96
Arthur, Duke of Connaught and Strathearn (1850-1942), 38
Awoonor-Gordon, Arnold, 109

Beatles, The, 15
Beatrice, Princess (1857-1944), 38, 108
Beecroft, John (1790-1854), 23, 24
Behanzin, King of Dahomey (1844-1906), 18
Blanke, John, 12
Bonetta, Sarah Forbes (c.1843-1880), 7-9, 15, 16; early life, 33; rescued by Forbes, 34; first journey to England, 34-35; visits to Windsor, 36-7, 93-5; settled with Forbes family, 38, 41; Queen Victoria sends back to Africa because of ill-health, 42; return to Africa, 45-58; return to England, 61-62; settled with Schoen family, 63-69; at wedding of Princess Royal, 67; and proposal of marriage from James Davies, 72-74; at Brighton with Miss Welsh, 75-78, 80-81; writes to Queen Victoria after death of Duchess of Kent, 79; marries James, 82-84; married life in Africa, 91; teaching career, 92-93, 94; birth of children, 93, 95; final illness, 96-97; death, 98-99; memorial at Lagos, 100

Brewer, Jane, 76
Brown, Dr, 42

Cardoneso, Catalina de, 11
Catherine, Queen, formerly Princess Catherine of Aragon (1485-1536), 11, 12
Charlotte, Queen (1744-1818), 13
Coker, Jacob Kehinda, 106
Coleman, Jenna (b.1986), 7
Coleridge-Taylor, Samuel (1875-1912), 15, 108
Conroy, Sir John (1786-1854), 37
Conroy, Victoire, 37
Crowther, Abigail, 52
Crowther, Asano, 52
Crowther, Reverend Samuel Ajayi (c.1809-1891), 52, 57, 63, 93

Dahomey, 18-25, 33, 39, 46-48, 54-57, 61, 79
Davies, Arthur (b.1871), 95
Davies, Captain James Pinson Labulo (1828-1906), 74; first meets Sarah, 58; early life, 72; considered as husband for Sarah, 73-74, 77; proposes to Sarah, 81; wedding, 84; married life in Africa, 91; business and political interests, 95-6; erects monument to Sarah in Lagos, 100; later business ventures, third marriage and death, 106-107
Davies, Stella (b.1873), 95
Davies, Victoria Matilda, later Randle (1863-1920), 93-5, 98, 106-8
Dicker, Reverend E., 62-63
Dudley Ward, Freda (Winifred) (1894-1983), 11

Edward VII, King (1841-1910); lack of racial prejudice, 10
Edward VIII, King (1894-1972), 11
Edward, Duke of Kent (1767-1820), 37
Elizabeth I, Queen (1533-1603), 12
Elizabeth II, Queen (b.1926), 11

Fanque, Pablo (William Darby) (1810-1871), 15

Forbes, Frederick Edwyn (1819-1851), 46, 99; and mission to Dahomey to help end slave trade, 18, 20-26; rescues Sarah and takes her to England, 31-37; gives her a home with his family, 38-39, 41; and Sarah's return to Africa, 47; book on mission to Dahomey, 47, 54, 82; death and burial at sea, 48
Forbes, Captain [brother of Frederick], 83-84
Forbes, Mary, 35, 53, 62-64, 67
Frederick III, German Emperor (1831-1888), 10, 67

George I, King (1660-1727), 12
George III, King (1738-1820), 13, 37
Gezo, King of Dahomey (d.1858), 19-23, 25, 31-32, 35-36, 48, 56-57, 61
Goodwin, Daisy (b.1961), 7
Griffith, Sir Brandford (1855-1928), 106

Hamilton-Gordon, Sir Arthur, 1st Baron Stanmore (1829-1912), and Lady, 16
Henre, Henry, 12
Henry VII, King (1457-1509), 12
Henry VIII, King (1491-1547), 12
Henry, Duke of Cornwall (b. & d. 1511), 12
Hibbert, Christopher (1924-2008), 8

Johnson, James, 107

Kalakaua, King of Hawaii (1836-1891), 10
Karim, Abdul (1863-1909), 9

Leopold I, King of the Belgians (1790-1865), 80
Leopold, Prince, Duke of Albany (1853-1884), 38, 94
Longford, Elizabeth (1906-2002), 8
Louis XIV, King of France (1638-1715), 14
Louis, Grand Duke of Hesse and the Rhine (1837-1892), 68

MacCarthy, Charles, 47
Madragana, 13

Maria Theresa, Queen of France (1660-1683), 14
Marie Anne of France, Princess (b. & d. 1664), 14
Mayall, John Jabez (1813-1901), 37-38
Mehemet, 12-13
Morrison, Shelby, 9
Mustapha, 12-3
Myers, Walter Dean (1937-2014), 8, 9, 109

Nichol, Reverend, 84

Olusoga, David (b.1970), 9

Palmerston, Henry John Temple, Viscount (1784-1865), 19, 23
Phipps, Sir Charles (1801-66), 68; and responsibility for Sarah, 38-39, 45, 48, 53-54; and Sarah's betrothal, 74
Phipps, Margaret, Lady (d.1874), 39, 41, 47, 58, 75, 80; letters to and from Sarah, 61, 63-64, 66-67, 76; and Sarah's betrothal, 73-74
Ponsonby, Sir Henry (1825-1895), 11, 14

Ramsay, Allan (1713-1784), 18
Randle, Beatrice, 108
Randle, John (1855-1928), 106-108
Randle, Romanes Adewale (John), 108
Randle, Thomas, 107
Randle, Victoria Matilda, *see under* Davies
Rappaport, Helen (b.1947), 9
Reffle, Catherine Kofoworola, 106

Salisbury, Robert Cecil, Marquess of (1830-1903), 10
Sass, Miss, 51-56, 58, 62
Schoen, Reverend James (b.1803), 63-65
Schoen, Elizabeth (b.1816), 61, 63-64, 66, 75, 77, 80, 83; Sarah's letters to, 73, 79, 94-96
Schoen, Fredcrick, 68
Scott, Sir Walter (1771-1832), 14
Serrano, Matilda Bonifacio, 73

Sierra Leone, 15, 45-50, 52, 55-57, 61-62, 67, 72, 91-92, 107-109
Simon, Barbara, 76
Slave Trade Act (1807), 17
Slavery Abolition Act (1833), 17
Sombre, David Ochterlony Dyce (1808-51), 15
Souza, Margarita de Castro e, 13
St Aubyn, Giles (1925-2015), 8
Stockmar, Christian Friedrich (1787-1863), 14

Twumasi-Ankrah, Nana Kofi, 11

Venn, Reverend Henry (1796-1873), 50, 57, 91, 95; early career, 45; responsibility for Sarah, 50, 53-54; and James Davies' proposal to Sarah, 72, 74, 81; at Sarah and James' wedding, 84
Victoria, Queen (1819-1901) 7, 10, 16, 18, 32, 38, 43, 49, 50, 56, 58, 67, 73, 92, 108; lack of racial prejudice, 9, 66, 109; ancestry, 13; Sarah offered as gift to, 35-36; first meets Sarah, 36; early life, 37; and Sarah's subsequent visits to Windsor Castle, Buckingham and St James's Palaces, 39, 41, 64, 82, 93-95; decides to send Sarah back to Africa on health grounds, 42, 44-45; pays for Sarah's education and sends her presents, 51, 53-54, 65; orders Sarah back to England, 61-62; and James Davies' proposal to Sarah, 74-76, 81, 83; and deaths of Duchess of Kent and Prince Albert, 79-80; becomes Victoria Davies' godmother, 93; and Sarah's last illness and death, 98-99; death, and financial provision for Victoria Davies, 106-107
Victoria, Princess Royal, later Princess Frederick William of Prussia, subsequently Empress Frederick (1840-1901), 67, 68
Victoria, Duchess of Kent (1786-1861), 79

Weintraub, Stanley (b.1929), 8
Wells, Nathaniel, 15
Welsh, Sophie, 75-76
Welsh, William, 76

Wilkinson, Miss, 62
Wilson, A.N. (b.1950), 8
Woodham-Smith, Mrs Cecil (1896-1977), 8

ALSO BY JOHN VAN DER KISTE

Royal and historical biography

Frederick III (1981)
Queen Victoria's Family: A Select Bibliography (1982)
Dearest Affie [with Bee Jordaan] (1984)
  - revised edition, *Alfred* (2014)
Queen Victoria's Children (1986)
Windsor and Habsburg (1987)
Edward VII's Children (1989)
Princess Victoria Melita (1991)
George V's Children (1991)
George III's Children (1992)
Crowns in a Changing World (1993)
Kings of the Hellenes (1994)
Childhood at Court 1819-1914 (1995)
Northern Crowns (1996)
King George II and Queen Caroline (1997)
The Romanovs 1818-1959 (1998)
Kaiser Wilhelm II (1999)
The Georgian Princesses (2000)
Dearest Vicky, Darling Fritz (2001)
Royal Visits to Devon & Cornwall (2002)
Once a Grand Duchess [with Coryne Hall] (2002)
William and Mary (2003)
Emperor Francis Joseph (2005)
Sons, Servants & Statesmen (2006)
A Divided Kingdom (2007)
William John Wills (2011)

The Prussian Princesses (2014)
The Big Royal Quiz Book (2014)
Prince Henry of Prussia (2015)
The last German Empress (2015)
Princess Helena (2015)
Charlotte and Feodora (2015)
Dictionary of Royal Biographers (2015)
The first German Empress (2016)
Daughter of Prussia (2017)
Of Royalty and Drink (2017)
The End of the German Monarchy (2017)
The Dukes of Clarence (2018)

Local history and true crime

Devon Murders (2006)
Devonshire's Own (2007)
Cornish Murders [with Nicola Sly] (2007)
A Grim Almanac of Devon (2008)
Somerset Murders [with Nicola Sly] (2008)
Cornwall's Own (2008)
Plymouth, History and Guide (2009)
A Grim Almanac of Cornwall (2009)
West Country Murders [with Nicola Sly] (2009)
Jonathan Wild (2009)
Durham Murders & Misdemeanours (2009)
Surrey Murders (2009)
Berkshire Murders (2010)
More Cornish Murders [with Nicola Sly] (2010)
Ivybridge & South Brent Through Time [with Kim Van der Kiste] (2010)
Dartmoor from old photographs (2010)
A Grim Almanac of Hampshire (2011)
The Little Book of Devon (2011)
More Devon Murders (2011)
More Somerset Murders [with Nicola Sly] (2011)
The Plymouth Book of Days (2011)
The Little Book of Cornwall (2013)
Plymouth, a City at War 1914-45 (2014)

Music

Roxeventies (1982)
Singles File (1987)
Beyond the Summertime [with Derek Wadeson] (1990)
Gilbert & Sullivan's Christmas (2000)
Roy Wood (2014)
Jeff Lynne (2015)
Pop Pickers and Music Vendors (2016)
A Beatles Miscellany (2016)
We Can Swing Together (2017)
Electric Light Orchestra Song by Song (2017)
While You See a Chance (2018)

Fiction

The Man on the Moor (2004)
Olga and David (2014)
Elmore Sounds (2015)
Always There (2015)

Plays and verse

The Man on the Moor (2015)
A Mere Passing Shadow (2015)
Dartmoor and other places (2015)

For availability of the above titles, please refer to Amazon.co.uk/Amazon.com

Made in the USA
Middletown, DE
01 December 2018